Digital Magazine Design
with case studies

WITHDRAWN

Paul Honeywill
Daniel Carpenter

**intellect**™
Bristol. UK
Portland OR, USA

First published in Great Britain in 2003 by
intellect
PO Box 862, Bristol, BS99 1DE, UK

First published in USA in 2003 by
intellect
ISBS, 5804 N. E. Hassalo St, Portland, Oregon 97213-3644, USA

Copyright
Part 1 ©2003 Paul Honeywill
Part 2 ©2003 Jennifer Campbell, Becky Gadd, Daniel Carpenter,
Paul Prudden, May Yao and Alison Evans respectively

Consulting Editor: Masoud Yazdani
Copy Editor: Daniel Carpenter
Cover design: Paul Honeywill and Daniel Carpenter

A catalogue record for this book is available from the British
Library

ISBN 1-84150-086-0

Printed and bound in the UK by Cromwell Press, Wiltshire

Contents

Acknowledgements

The author and editor would like to thank the postgraduate students of the University of Plymouth Faculty of Arts and Education for their contributions, Jane Weston for her help and advice, and Phil Cutler and Nic Earle for their technical support.

Copyrights

Trademarks

Preface

Page design without the aid of a computer is almost unheard of these days, but there is still much to learn from the past by applying accepted principles to contemporary magazine design. Laying out pages before computers required a detailed understanding of the processes involved. The advent of desktop publishing has led to the removal of many of those processes which retained trade and professional specialisms, such as graphic design, typesetting and so on. Consequently, DTP became branded as a lower order of design by some professionals. In many cases it was a lack of design knowledge that gave dismissive ammunition to the elite few who regarded DTP in this way. In its defense, it was not the technology that reflected the design quality; it was its availability to anybody who wanted to 'desktop publish'.

Contemporary publications can have very complex designs and by analyzing their structure and components it is possible to understand and apply these methodologies to other areas of design such as leaflets, posters and so on. Magazines are a good starting point because they know who their audience is and are designed accordingly.

The first part of this book will equip you with a foundation of knowledge that will allow you to develop appropriate design skills by understanding what to look for, as opposed to being shown examples of clever designs which you could reproduce only by step-by-step copying without knowing why. The second part of the book contains a series of case studies by postgraduate Publishing students who have used the first part of the book as reference. None of these students have a design background, but because technology allows one person to perform many tasks within the publishing process it is important for them to have this grounding. Each case study is concerned with text, image, design and the way a reader perceives published material through legibility and editorial suitability for its intended use. Through understanding the relationship between these factors and being capable of making informed judgments, the student is able to make a critical and analytical evaluation of all publishable material. This is achieved through the analysis of a magazine publication's physical architecture, graphic and typographic personality, method of production and intended readership.

The students were required to develop the case study by identifying a magazine which was relevant to their interest and worthy of further study by devising a small-scale investigation or project to carry out. The students who have written the case studies are not designers, but they will be expected to work with design and edit text in their chosen career as publishers. In this respect, it is the intention of this book to equip the reader with the tools of design and to give examples of how to achieve good practice in applying these tools to contemporary printed material.

Paul Honeywill
University of Plymouth

Stepping up to the Interface

There are many page-design programs. However, the principles of stepping up to the interface are almost always the same. Students who have undertaken the case studies in the final section of this book have all used QuarkXPress. Most interface references will be to that program.

Volume low

Volume high

You understand the metaphor that the computer volume control uses to describe the real world; when you adjust the volume control this is exactly what you expect. Learning to use your chosen page-design software is no different.

If you are relatively new to using a computer to design a page, this chapter suggests an initial approach. When learning a specific page-design program, it is always best to understand the real-world metaphor that the software uses to describe the tools and techniques that a graphic designer would use. I have always found it useful for the student to understand how a program describes the computer interface as a working graphic studio, and then position the student in relation to the computer and the design. Learning software on its own is insufficient, even though page-design training often tends to be confined to software learning. Understanding comes from your knowledge of the metaphor that the computer uses to describe the real world. If you, as a student, understand the logic of the metaphor and its functions, you are then equipped to learn, develop and exploit the nature of digital design.

You learn to navigate through the real world by recognizing representational symbols that describe objects, and the actions that you should take as a consequence. You are able to adjust the sound level on your computer with relative ease because the graphic representation of the volume control is familiar. An unfamiliar image would not enable you to understand its function. Learning to use any page-design program is no different. By unpacking and understanding these processes you should be able to familiarize yourself each time your chosen software package is upgraded or undergoes a major redesign of its interface and functions.

By doing so you can extend this approach and apply this method to any software. This introductory chapter could be used for any program which has been written to operate in a windows environment for either Macintosh or PC. What is important is your understanding of what the action words mean and how the desktop metaphor of noun and verb represent these actions. When using the image-manipulation software Photoshop, a photographer would understand the function of a Noise Filter for Despeckling or altering the radius of the Median because it relates to a real-life process that he or she is familiar with. A graphic designer will understand the language of typography used as the action verbs within page design programs, such as track (overall space between letters and words) and kern (individual space between letters).

The nature of design using a computer allows you to reflect upon human perception, which tends to be altered through the new possibilities that the digital capability of a computer can offer. By exploring the potential of design using computers, new opportunities can be established. There are three distinct concepts you need to understand to effectively use page-design programs as a tool:

- The software object/action computer interface is a metaphor for working in a graphic design studio;
- Knowledge of design, its principles and its terminology are just as important when using a computer to design as they ever were;
- Certain elements of design remain constant, while other elements can be exploited using a computer.

Understanding the desktop metaphor and being familiar with computer interfaces encourages you to make the most of new opportunities. Pointing and selecting becomes inseparable from the desktop assumption that people are inquisitive; they want to learn, especially if the environment appears recognizable and engaging. With most page-design programs the design studio metaphor creates an interface that allows you to use the tools of graphic design. To operate the computer you look for objects that are familiar. These objects suggest their function; even though the language and description of functionality needs only to be approximate and not exact (for more on interface iconography, go to www.w3icons.com).

The Interface as a Metaphor for the Real World

Successful computer operation owes much to the rules of Isotype (International System Of TYpographic Picture Education). The importance of Isotype with regard to computer interaction is the collaboration between Ogden, who was the inventor of Basic English (British American Scientific International Commercial), and Neurath. Ogden had asked Neurath to publish an outline of his visual language; Neurath agreed if Ogden also allowed Basic to be combined with Isotype in an additional book, *Basic by Isotype*. Ogden's Basic English contained eight hundred and fifty core words which were mainly nouns or verbs.

O. Neurath, *Basic by Isotype*, Psych Minatures General Series (London: Kegan Paul, 1936).

These two fundamental paradigms of object and action are central to the computer desktop metaphor. The decision to publish an explanation of Isotype and a version underpinned by selective language is crucial to the way in which the system was understood and adopted for other uses. The introduction of the 1980 facsimile *International picture language/Internationale Bildersprache* cites instructions for telephone systems, traffic signs and so on. It was not until January 1983 that the concept of icons as a plausible interface between user and computer was made possible with the development and launch of the Apple Lisa by Steve Jobs and Steve Wozniak.

O. Neurath, *International picture language/ Internationale Bildersprache*, a facsimile reprint of the 1936 English edition, forward by Robin Kinross, Psyche Miniatures General Series (London: Kegan Paul and the Department of Typography & Graphic Communication, University of Reading, 1980).

Before the development of an intuitive interface all human/computer interaction was through command-line instructions. This required a high level of computer understanding. Computers were for computing and not for ordinary working tasks. Many graphic communication systems have evolved from the Isotype/Basic method, and it is only natural that the Apple Lisa developed the object/action interface. Learning complex Boolean logic was no longer required to operate a computer. People with real needs could now execute complex code sequences without the need to recall correct command-lines. For the PC, the metaphor was not truly complete until the introduction of Windows 95. Both Macintosh and PC operating systems have now become indistinguishable from each other; the interface metaphor is complete. When the same page-design programs have been launched on either platform there is little or no difference in how they look and function.

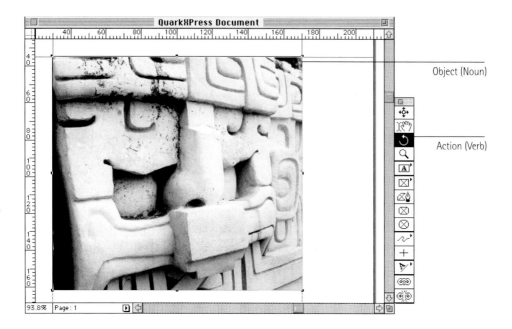

Object (Noun)

Action (Verb)

However, it was the Macintosh operating system that set the standards for computing as we now know it. Apple's *Human Interface Guidelines: The Apple Desktop Interface* (1987), states that objects and their actions which combine representational image and language operation, allow the user to 'rely on recognition, not recall; they shouldn't have to remember anything a computer already knows'. Human computer interaction could now happen through an intuitive interface that iconically represented familiar objects found in the real world. The computer could now do real work for ordinary needs. All page-design software now operates within this metaphor. Tools such as the Bézier tool (French curves) can be found in the real world and designers use the same tools in a studio to draw uneven curves as they do on screen.

Neurath perceived Isotype as a helpful visual language underpinned with key basic words. Visual language alone is insufficient because representational meaning can only be approximate. Therefore, like with Isotype/Basic, each object on the computer desktop is named. However, written words become redundant if the user is unfamiliar with the language. A system

Object selection (the picture) and then the action (rotation, crop scale and so on).

Apple, *Human Interface Guidelines: The Apple Desktop Interface* (Boston: Addison-Wesley, 1987).

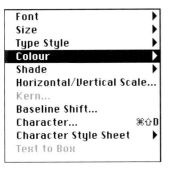

Font	▶
Size	▶
Type Style	▶
Colour	▶
Shade	▶
Horizontal/Vertical Scale...	
Kern...	
Baseline Shift...	
Character...	⌘⇧D
Character Style Sheet	▶
Text to Box	

Action (Verb) as
Basic language.

where images are representational would allow the user to become familiar with their own basic word usage that underpins the picture. Neurath explains that 'a man coming into a strange country without knowledge of the language is uncertain where to get his ticket at the station or the harbour, where to put his boxes, how to make use of the telephone in the telephone box, where to go in the post office. But if he sees pictures by the side of strange words, they will put him on the right way'. For the first-time user, the clue to functionality within page-design software is suggested through iconic representation. Pull-down menus contain written language; as a metaphor they share no resemblance with their restaurant counterpart. They provide the choice of action after the object has been chosen. The menu as metaphor allows you to 'pull-down' menus and to browse these actions.

This consistent approach has been uniformly adopted for the development of programs for the PC. By learning one application you already know how other applications will be controlled. As long as you understand the basic vocabulary, you will not be hindered. The menu bar remains consistent between programs; File and Edit become stable actions located to the top of the bar, while other actions may be specific to a particular program. At all times you have a familiar reference point. Navigation on the desktop becomes icon selection and the available Basic word action. You are denied non-applicable actions within page-design software; the Basic text becomes 'greyed-out'. Computer navigation within page-design software expands the primary desktop metaphor encouraging you to 'see-and-point', highlighting the object and then the action. After the noun/verb relationship has been learned, advanced interaction can be learned through the pre-programmed keyboard shortcut commands.

The *Apple Programmer's Introduction to the Apple IIGS* reminds the programmer of the importance of graphic images. It returns your attention to the human-interface guideline and states that 'objects on screens should be simple and clear, and they should have visual fidelity (that is, they should look like what they represent). The desktop is the primary metaphor in the Apple Desktop interface'. Regardless of the underlying code, if any part of the two fundamental paradigms of recognition and action are not

Apple, *Apple Programmer's introduction to the Apple IIGS* (Boston: Addison-Wesley, 1988).

underpinned by concrete metaphors and Basic language, accessibility becomes difficult.

Central to the Isotype philosophy is the belief that images reduced to a common representation have greater effect than mere words. Images aid intuition and create a human/computer interface that is centred on you. Interface designers recognize that human activity is complex and that many factors are still unknown, but the common recognition is that people want to achieve tasks without the need to understand navigation through exact command-lines, especially at the first stage of acquiring new knowledge.

Underlying Principles

Knowledge gives you choice. By knowing the basic rules you can control the design of the printed page.

The proceeding chapters explore the key factors that you should consider. They have been written to help you identify basic rules and understand how these rules are applied using page-design software.

Pre-digital magazine design is distinctive for its rigid column structures. There was, in the days before computers, very little margin for error within the typographic specification for the page, because the layout depended upon physically cutting and pasting elements onto a board. Digital page design allows for the manipulation of all the elements on a page, resulting in more complex and ambitious structures. Control is still central in designing any page and there are three distinctive parts to effectively using the digital medium as a design tool. Designers and printers use page-design programs that reflect the terminology of previous technologies (cut and paste is a self-explanatory example, track and kern is not). Designers and printers are familiar with the names and can therefore use them accordingly. The following chapters describe good practice when handling digital files, the basics of design and the terminology that design uses.

The language of design, and design itself, has always been influenced by the technology that allows you to communicate your ideas. The methods used to chisel letters in stone and cast individual letters from lead have altered the perception of what design should or can be through the available technology of that time. Using a computer is no different, it creates new opportunities to communicate, and in so doing alters the perception of what design is. Before you begin to exploit digital design you will need to be aware of the conventions that have been established. Some of these conventions continue to be adapted to meet the needs of new digital technologies. So before you can organize text and images into effective communication you will need to know some basic perceptual rules.

There is nothing to say what you should or should not do; this is not engineering, where the design has structural implications. With page design there is no bridge to fall down. However, other people's perception will determine whether or not you are successful.

Approaching Design Development

Design tasks for print happen for a purpose. The person for whom you undertake a design task will want to disseminate material for an audience. People who want your knowledge may vary from those that need the occasional newsletter or fanzine, to the professional magazine publisher who will not continue before certain conditions have been satisfied. Publishing has developed sophisticated methods of production from the initial idea to the point-of-sale. It is important for you to know how a professional magazine publisher thinks, before being able to adapt that model for other tasks within magazine design. Not only will you need to master technology and understand design, but you will also be required to assess the appropriateness of the design for the intended audience.

Task originator	Do people want or need this publication?
	Who are these people? Can they be defined?
You	Access to all the material such as text and images?
	Has all the material been received as promised?
Task originator	How many people will actually receive the publication?
	Can enough be sold to make the publication viable?

The second, third and fourth points above are crucial for you. They define the intended readership and the availability of the material, and neither should be in doubt before the design process begins. You will need to decide upon the media format of the material, such as transparencies, computer text files and so on.

You will also need to establish points of agreement for the workflow. This will help to eliminate problems at a later stage. For example, if the text has been agreed and then changes are made, errors can occur. The main points of contact and agreement will vary according to your task (depending on the print production route and the delivery of the work for distribution), but the overall model holds true and should be adapted by you. Begin the work when an agreement has been reached. An overly specific brief will

Dorothy Goslett, *The Professional Practice of Design*, 3rd Edition (London: Batsford, 1984).

restrict creative input, while a brief that is not specific enough could result in you starting from the beginning again. To avoid this, Dorothy Goslett suggests in *The Professional Practice of Design* that the ideal person for you to undertake work for knows what they want, and will allow creative freedom to enhance your outcome.

By understanding the relationship between you and the design-task originator, and appreciating the reason for publication, you can direct your knowledge of design and technology towards the audience. At this stage thought must be given to the personality of the publication, and your thinking must be shared with the task originator. This allows your design to evolve through their perception of the intended audience. The focused aim of the design is to stimulate the reader, be applicable to the audience, retain legibility and work within output limitations. This requires self-criticism and a disciplined approach to working methods.

The problem with learning magazine design is that it can be difficult to establish a holistic approach, without having gone through the process several times, and understanding that many decisions are grouped together and experiential. Most designers spend hours sketching out possible solutions that might work. Each series of quick sketches builds on the strength of the previous ones, eliminating the weak points until a solution has been achieved that satisfies all the constraints of audience need and production cost.

Analysis, synthesis and decision completes the first cycle of thought, each cycle adds another level of design understanding through reflection. The philosopher Ryle, in *The Concept of the Mind*, considered the cycle of thought as 'very much a matter of drills and skills'. Successive cycles build knowledge, and without critical reflection, a formulaic solution becomes the danger. To avoid this you need to:

Gilbert Ryle, *The Concept of Mind* (London: Hutchinson, 1949).

Analyze	Who are the intended readership and what are the constraints?
Synthesize	Integrate the needs and constraints.
Decide	Implement the design.

In *The Five Day Course in Thinking*, Edward de Bono warned against formulas and suggested that it is 'more important to be skillful in thinking than to be stuffed with facts'. In short, when considering digital design, each solution can be different, just like with design methodologies before computers. Digital technology has made thousands of typefaces immediately available, allowing expressive freedom for some and confusion for others. Expressive freedom can only be obtained by knowing which factors influence the design.

Edward de Bono, *The Five Day Course in Thinking* (London: Allen Lane, 1968).

The same task can have multiple solutions; there is no 'right way', and to apply a formula that has worked before would be to deny yourself the understanding that comes with working through the design process. In the proceeding chapters you must consider what was good pre-digital design practice, and what computers can offer to enrich magazine design.

Pen and Paper

Digital manipulation means that you can have direct creative interaction with your design. However, you still need to plan because complex designs require various data files that need to be managed during the development of the design on screen. The majority of the thinking process should have been completed before launching an application, as the computer is best suited for refining the design. By starting the work directly on a computer you are limited to your understanding of the technology, restricting your creative ability. When using software at an early stage of the learning process, the first solution might become precious and change become uncomfortable and undesirable.

Keep your ideas achievable. The accessibility of this technology can allow for an unchecked riot of ideas which will confuse and not clarify the main idea that you are trying to convey.

This sounds like a step backwards, but at the initial stage simple tools such as pen and paper are still the best method of expressing creative ideas. Work with thumbnails (small sketches), remembering that the aim is to make it easy for the reader to understand the points being made; thumbnails will allow you to add emphasis to these points. Thumbnails can be erased and replaced, building the design to gain the required emphasis. At a later stage, when you have grasped these principles, the role of paper might be reduced to the production of thumbnails as a visual map for your own reference.

Design your publication with set standards. This will allow your reader to recognize parts of the page for what they are, sub-headings, captions, quotes and so on. At the computing stage this information can be applied to the style sheets.

As an initial exercise to help you progress beyond small sketches, build a kit by printing out images, headings (in various sizes), and some text. Make sure that your layout area has a border so that you know the relationship between the paper edges and your elements. This kit will allow you to keep the design fluid and also aid in the thinking process. By physically cutting and pasting you have full control of the publication's appearance, and working with paper allows you to experiment visually, while retaining a clear focus on your readership.

Finally, when you begin to apply your design within a page-layout application there is a striking difference between creative outcomes from different technologies. The technology itself imparts certain characteristics onto the work. What you might have worked out on paper will look different on the screen. Try not to fight it; this is where digital environments can enhance the design through the ease of direct manipulation. Good design is developed through a series of re-workings, each refining the design until the desired outcome has been reached.

Working On Screen

Proper planning on paper should also include the role of technology. When the design has been worked to a satisfactory level on paper, include notes for image sizes, the use of typography, and any other design elements that you plan to use. More detail now will require less memory recall at a later stage. This information will be required when establishing page formats and style sheets, as with pre-digital publications that had a sheet of style instructions to ensure consistency from one issue to the next. It is at this point that decisions can be taken regarding the digitization of any images. How you acquire and use images will depend on the specification of your computer. Having insufficient processing power or RAM (Random Access Memory) for many high-resolution images in a working document can be equivalent to using the exhaust pipe to turn your car around, instead of using the steering wheel.

You might consider sending your images to a reprographic bureau or scanning them yourself, depending on your design. If the approximate size of each image is known, sending them to a

```
┌─────────────────────────────────────────────────────────────┐
│                            Print                              │
│  Print Style:  Document ▼                                     │
│                                                               │
│  Copies: █      Pages: All              ▼  ( Range Separators...) │
│  ┌─────────┬───────┬────────┬─────────┬─────────┐            │
│  │Document │ Setup │ Output │ Options │ Preview │            │
│  └─────────┴───────┴────────┴─────────┴─────────┘            │
│  ☐ Separations          ☐ Spreads         ☐ Collate          │
│  ☒ Include Blank Pages   ☒ Thumbnails      ☐ Back to Front    │
│  Page Sequence: All ▼                                         │
│  Registration:  Off ▼    Bleed:  0 mm                        │
│  Tiling:        Off ▼    Overlap:          ☐ Absolute Overlap │
│                                                               │
│  (Page Setup...) (Printer...) │ (Capture Settings)(Cancel)(Print) │
└─────────────────────────────────────────────────────────────┘
```

QuarkXPress will allow you to output thumbnails to give you a clear overview of the design.

bureau will allow you to manipulate the low-resolution thumbnails (OPI or Open Prepress Images) returned by them. Another alternative is to scan the images yourself as FPO (For Position Only) images. If, however, you intend to manipulate these illustrations within an image-processing program you will require the bureau to scan the images and return the LIVE image (files containing the data for the final printing resolution) for manipulation. The advantage of using a bureau is that they can digitize a range of different media formats at your required resolution.

Digital files need to be organized for ease of transportation at the final stage; and for the practical reasons of electronic pick-up (the page-design document will create routes to imported image files). When all your material is in a digital format, place the files in a folder that clearly describes your work. Create additional folders for images, text and the page make-up documents. Place these folders into the first folder. A well-organized hierarchy of folders will ensure that files are not forgotten at a later stage, when they leave your desktop for output by another computer. This organization of work also helps you locate files when text and images are imported into your document.

The next task is to establish the format of your document and the required number of pages. Adding or deleting pages at a later stage can disrupt page linking in some page make-up programmes. After establishing the format you can set your style sheets so that all imported text can be readily converted into headings, sub-headings, body text and so on. Working with thumbnails does not end at the paper stage of the design process. On a large document you cannot see all aspects of the design; as with paper sketches it is important to output computer thumbnails to give you this overview.

Not only has desktop technology combined many processes, it has also introduced the possibility of different media outcomes. This might need to be included in your design plan. Dissemination of knowledge is no longer only about paper, other digital formats might be required for CD-ROM or the World Wide Web. This is where digital technologies really extend the possibilities; the original content can be used as the base material for many solutions. Allowing for this at the planning stage will determine different file destinations and document types if unnecessary re-workings are to be avoided later. Your small thumbnail sketches then become supplemented and overlaid with Web maps and multimedia storyboards. Each medium is different, however, and should not be confused with simply viewing the publication through a screen. It is not just a matter of changeover; nobody makes videos of still text and pictures.

Who Should Be Responsible?

Originally, simple tasks such as page layout were taken over by the person with multiple skills to exploit the multi-tasking nature of the technology. Within magazine publishing, the layout designer and editor were always separate people. Now the requirement is for a production editor who can design the page using the style sheets and document templates, and edit the text as well. Mainstream publishing might call upon the services of a design agency or individual to establish templates and style sheets, but it is the production editor that implements the design on an issue-to-issue basis. Without this understanding the democratic nature of digital design cannot progress beyond desktop publishing to the quality of design that is demonstrated in the magazines on sale in any high street shop.

The latter point has not been lost on publishing courses. The editor can now implement the design of the page and prepare the publication for printing: one person now has the opportunity to make many mistakes. There is greater opportunity for skills to be diluted and there are many skills within the process. A magazine is usually created through the co-operation of many people. Each will view the publication differently; the words, the design, printing, binding, and so on. The technology provides the temptation to make any ongoing publication the sole domain of the computer user who understands a page make-up program. The instigation of any design modification undertaken, however, should be the jurisdiction of the person who understands design and its terminology. They can reflect objectively and make informed decisions, applying a knowledge of design and how it is implemented through digital technology.

People who require regular printing, such as a magazine publisher, will have agreements with paper suppliers, reprographic houses and printers. They will work within set specifications, making each supplier compatible with the others. This in turn affects how many pages can be printed together (imposition), before folding into a section, and so on. Paper, film, plate and press allow for final checks on the end product. Technology streamlines these processes; the computer can now output directly to plate or digital press, shifting further responsibility to the desktop. You can see, then, that technology does not relieve the responsibility of the magazine designer; it makes their job all the more important.

Setting up the Page

Workflow should be organized so that the route of each file is easily managed.

Page-design documents, text files, LIVE images, FPO images and OPI images should all have a separate folder within your digital 'job bag.'

This chapter will show you how to structure a magazine by explaining the reasoning behind the design. By knowing how to analyze a high street magazine you can make informed decisions about the publication you are designing. Human perception tends to change gradually through exposure to new ideas, especially the ways in which we perceive the layout of the page within advanced consumer cultures. You might note that most of the case studies identify changes in the design of their respective magazines, either as a complete makeover (but as not to alienate the user) or as gradual and continual. Before computers were in regular use, the different parts of the publishing process tended to be defined by what people did. Part of the design would involve making sure that the copy-fit/cast-off (a calculation of how many pages ordinary text would cover when changed into a typeface) was correct, before any marked-up copy (the ordinary text with typographic style instructions) was sent for typesetting. The returned galley (continuous typeset text) would be physically cut and pasted as artwork, and column structure would be easily identifiable. Digital technology allows for complex structures within contemporary magazine design. Their structure might not be so easily detectable at first inspection.

As explained in the previous chapter, pre-digital technologies involved many specialisms. As both typesetter and designer were separate people the terms that described each other's requirements had to be exact. Columns were mostly drawn-up with regular measurements because of the problems of estimating where the text would finish. Artwork surfaces would be hand drawn to include all non-printing grid structures (guidelines) reproduced in blue (blue was not sensitive to lithographic film). Type was then cut and pasted into position. All elements (text and image) of the design were stored in a 'job bag' or documents folder.

Page-design software interfaces owe much to the working methods of a previous technology. The desktop becomes a metaphor for the drawing board complete with a full set of tools. Text is edited within a word-processing program and images are manipulated and sized within an imaging program. The format of the publication and the page extent will have been decided before these elements are imported into the page-design software. Now the on-screen design becomes artwork and remains fluid. Instead of a collection of physical items, all the design elements are in a digital format, such as LIVE images: pictures scanned at the final printing resolution. FPO images scanned by you on a low-resolution desktop scanner will be rescanned at high-resolution for the final output. OPI thumbnails, which are small file-size images of the final scan, allow you to handle the image file with ease and will be replaced by the LIVE high-resolution file for final output. Your working documents folder should contain folders for these items.

After your design has been resolved on paper and before you place any elements within a page-design program, the page format and your personal preferences should be the first task, followed by the page furniture (page numbers and running heads). Unlike traditional methods, digital design allows you to manipulate the entire page and any design that is not planned first can, and probably will, suffer. In this respect the grid structure (format) is one of the most important design features at your disposal. It defines the selective positions for the four basic elements of design on the page: headings, body text, images and white space.

The grid also provides a consistent framework for manipulating these different graphic elements, maintaining page-to-page cohesion. Grids vary according to the kind of publication, books normally have one grid throughout, whereas a magazine will often have five, or as many as twelve plus, different grid structures. In a more complex publication multiple grids allow the reader to distinguish between the various sections. Whether the publication is single column or a mix of multiple columns, they all have one common aim, and that is to avoid static balance in relation to the page edges.

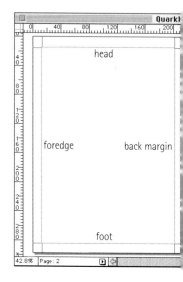

Parts of the left-hand (verso) page.

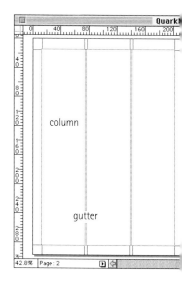

Page grid structure (format).

The optical centre of the page is higher than the mathematical. Preview your page on screen to judge by eye without the interference of guides.

Magazine pages are normally viewed as pairs. If you consider that the grid is the framework in which the elements of your design are located, then the back margin (the folding middle of a publication) should be closest to the inside fold. This is because space in the middle increases when the pages are viewed together. Also, any element placed on the page at the mathematical centre, appears to be below the centre, being pulled downwards. If the element is adjusted by the eye to appear central (optical centre), mathematically the element will be above the central position. This is why the judgment of your eye should be relied upon and not the mathematical decisions of a computer. This also applies to the smallest elements of any page design; even the crossbars (horizontal strokes) of upper case E and lower case e characters are always above the mathematical centre. If you look closely at the *serif* characters (bottom left) static balance has been avoided. The *serifs* on opposite sides of a letter are often not exact mirror images. Your mind demands variation in what the eye perceives to remain alert. Most magazines use a *serif* typeface for the main body text for this reason. Applying these fundamentals to the grid will help to keep your reader stimulated.

For single column books the largest margin should always be at the foot (bottom) of the page, and the smallest margin should normally be the back margin (between pages). Visually, both back margins should be equal to the foredge margin (outside). Magazines where the foot is not the widest margin tend to give an appearance of the text falling off the page. The head margin (top) should be proportionately bigger than the back margin followed by the foredge margin. This gives you a sequence to follow that will avoid static balance and stimulate the reader's eye when your elements are imported into the page. Simply put:

3 o' clock is the smallest margin and then growing larger in an anti-clockwise direction; 12 o' clock, 9 o' clock and, finally, 6 o' clock is the largest margin.

The formula above describes the left-hand (verso) page. The right-hand (recto) page starts again from the centre and is followed around clockwise. These rules are an indication of the relationship

Mathematical centre and the different size of serifs.

between page edge and text for a single text column. At this point it is worth mentioning the classic proportions described by Jan Tschichold: margins should follow the ratio 2:3:4:6 and the page width and height should follow the ratio 2:3. It avoids static balance, and interrupts eye movement to stimulate the reader. This stimulation is what you need to achieve. Most page design programs have margin guides that default to a uniform border for all margins. Today most designs have many demands and differing purposes, and cannot afford the luxury of classical proportions. The illustration below demonstrates Tschichold's formula extended closer to the page edges.

It is important to give this kind of consideration to the main working area of the page, but it is also important to consider the internal structure of the grid in relation to the elements of your design. A well-considered grid will assist in the placing of your text and images. Your page format needs only millimetres difference to avoid static balance.

Columns Within the Grid

The next important addition to the grid is the columns contained within. Obviously this depends on the type of magazine and the final page size. On the large page format of a magazine, the single column becomes very difficult to read. If the line of text is too long your reader will have difficulty moving from line to line (more on this later).

A well-considered grid will allow you to position the elements of the design effectively. The element within the design that is most dependent on the grid and column structure is the type, and the least dependent is normally the images used in support of the text. In most cases you should design the column width for use with the text. One of the most useful formats is the three-column grid. This structure provides an orderly arrangement of elements, while maintaining their flexibility. It creates a strong flow line (top grid line) of elements, which alters page balance.

At 3 o' clock the two smallest inside margins face each other. Viewed together they should appear visually equal with the outside margin opposite at 9 o' clock, the margin at the bottom should be the next biggest margin at 6 o' clock and have sufficient

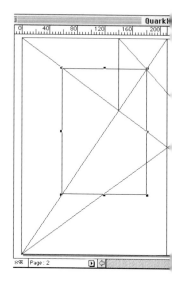

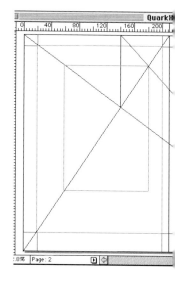

Top. Jan Tschichold's classical proportions are over-generous though they do demonstrate the relationship between text and page edges. *Below.* A more acceptable format.

When using images the three-column grid allows for greater flexibility and dramatic use of scale. Large images can be balanced against small images. This will give you the freedom to enliven the page and retain new interest for your reader each time they turn the page.

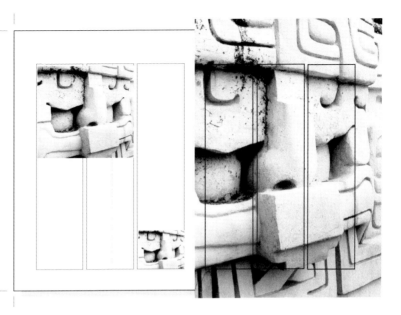

space so that the type does not appear to fall off the page. The margin at the top then becomes the biggest at 12 o' clock.

Magazines tend to have multiple columns of equal width, and narrow foredge margins. Both back margins equal the foredge margin, and white space gravitates upwards towards the head of the page. The sequence and spacing of the grid change. The head has more space than the foot. The relationship between the head and foot are dictated by the elements of the design, such as the visual greyness of the body type, position of the page furniture outside the grid, and so on. The advantage over the two-column structure is that images that fit within and adhere to the grid structure can be used in a greater number of combinations.

Both *serif* type and grid should have an asymmetrical quality, and, accordingly, columns do not necessarily have to be identical widths. The measure of any column can be unequal. The three-column can have two larger columns and one smaller column. These complex relationships allow for even greater flexibility: you can place an element that begins within one structure and finishes within another.

Two columns have fewer combinations of image use.

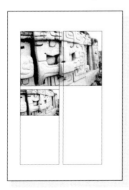

Once you have established a grid for your magazine, do not feel bound by its constraints. Text tends to conform to the grid, especially the body text. Images tend to anchor to the grid and then break through the grid. Large images at the bottom make the text at the top of the page visually fall forward unless they have been balanced with other images across your spread (double-page layout). Pages tend to balance well with contrasting large and small images; this again confirms a hierarchical order of how the page is read. Be dramatic with images; decide the order of importance and give your spread a focal point. This adds visual interest on your page yet still links it to the format.

The format should also allow ease of transition from one section to another, ensuring that your reader does not get lost. By being consistent with key elements you have taught the reader your rules of navigation.

Multiple Grids

Complex designs not only overlay one grid architecture over another, but can rotate the grid and reposition it within the same margins, or mirror the grid from left to right, especially if the column structure is asymmetrical. Different kinds of grid structures also help the reader to identify different parts of the magazine, as closer investigation of many high street magazines testifies. Grids are non-printing guidelines to help you position elements. Once they have been removed the publication takes on a visual coherence.

To understand these grids, take some tracing paper and position this on a magazine page that has a clear structure. As stated at the beginning of this chapter, contemporary magazines can be complex, so look for the simplest page as a starting point. Ignore images, headings and so on; look for the strong visual lines created by the body type. Draw all the outer grid margins of the page, and the columns within from the top of the grid to the bottom. Now place the grid template on other pages. This will determine if there is a new architecture. Because digital formats can allow individual changes to any column, look for clear change and not simply another column structure that is different by only a few millimetres. If a new structure is encountered, rotate and mirror your template to see if it has been used in a different way. If not, add this to your collection and start afresh. This very simple exercise will help to explain how the structure of the design has

Magazine design tends to require a high level of sophistication. The designer can achieve this by developing a complex grid system:

1) By creating an unequal column measure.
2) By reflecting these unequal measures from the right-hand page (recto) to the left-hand page (verso).
3) By using more than one grid.
4) By allowing elements to begin on one grid and finish on another.

Elements beginning in the two-column grid and finishing in the three-column grid.

been used and how it changes between sections.

Once you know what you are trying to achieve, you can challenge the traditional use of grids. If you analyze the structure of the magazine *Raygun* you cannot fail to notice that the publication appears to break every known rule. The designer knows the rules and has decided to develop a set unique to *Raygun* as part of the magazine's graphic personality. Each page is designed to illustrate the content, and pages become art within their own right.

You also need to consider the elements that exist outside of the grid. Technically, the furniture is part of the margin, but these elements establish a relationship with the grid and should be considered at the same time.

Outside the Grid

Running heads or folios should not interfere with the reading of the body text. All positions should isolate these elements from the grid.

Both running heads (the magazine or feature title running along the top of the page) and folios (page numbers and titles at the bottom) aid navigation. Both should be unobtrusive, yet easily identifiable for what they are. Page furniture can establish the name of the magazine, the date, volume number, and so on. Neither the running head nor the folio should interfere with the reading of the main text, or be large enough to be confused with headings or sub-headings. Space should be used in proportion to size; position and size depend on the publication.

How Will Pages Be Viewed?

Viewing elements in print and on screen is different; what you see is not necessarily what you get. Screen resolutions are lower than print resolutions, and on-screen type can appear too small to read at actual size. A comfortable viewing size is 12 pt, yet when printed the same type will appear too large. Using type management which has been set to preserve the best character shape will make the font appear smoother by anti-aliasing the pixels (adding grey or intermediate coloured pixels around the letter edge) but this does not resolve on-screen legibility of size.

When designing the grid, the computer screen can also give a false impression of the proportions of the page. Computer screens are flat; printed pages are not. Perfect-bound magazines will require more back margin space than their saddle-stitched

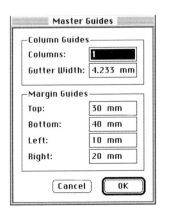

Page proportions.

(stapled) counterparts. Making a dummy (mock-up) will help to decide on the width of the margins. Manipulating the grid structure with a computer gives you the flexibility to make adjustments before you place any elements onto the page

Length of the Line

Before designing the page structure there are many combinations of measurement that you can set in your page-layout software. Most of the options that are available are based on the printers' measurement system, inches or metrification. QuarkXPress also allows you to set the measure in agates which is generally used for measuring vertical column depth in classified advertising. In the United Kingdom, North America and elsewhere, the points system (Pierre Fournier) is used. Other parts of the world that do not use this system have adopted the French Didot (François Didot) as their standard. Most page-design programs allow you to calibrate the measurement dialog for all these systems. None of these systems are compatible with each other. The Didot point is slightly larger than the English/North American point:

> The next two pages describe measurement. The logic of printing measurement can seem confusing. It is however, the language of the industry.

12 points make a pica
12 didot points make a cicero
12 didot = 12.9 pica

The UK has adopted a metric unit of measure which is being enforced by EU regulations. Paper now tends to be measured metrically, whereas America has retained inches for paper sizes. Even after metrification, the printing and publishing industry still retains imperial sizes, which they have to convert to metric. Inches do not readily convert, 32 by 42 inches becomes 812.8 by 1066.6 mm. When pages are imposed (planned into a printing order for the same sheet), sheet sizes that represent the inch measurements have been kept.

Measuring systems that have been based on the inch have traditionally used the point system because it corresponds closely to the imperial measurement. As a guide, 72 pts corresponds to one inch and is the PostScript and default value of most page-design programs (the exact traditional measure is considered as 1

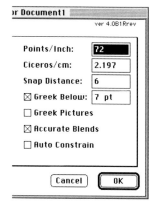

72 points per inch is the Postscript default value. The traditional non-digital value is slightly larger.

General document
preferences.

Default gutter widths are
normally 4.233 mm, which
is one pica-em.

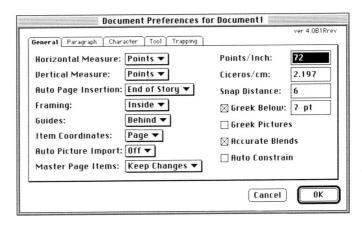

inch to 72.272 pts). However, this measure can be set at any value between 72 pts and 73 pts in 0.01 pt increments. The reduced size extends the column width and increases the line space, whereas the increased size tightens both. Professional page-design software re-calibrates point-to-inch measurement values. Any measurement that has been assigned a constant value before the adjustment will remain physically unaltered, but with a new re-calibrated typographic value based on the PostScript default. This is also true of the continental Didot system where the ciceros-to-centimetres conversion can also be set at any value between two and three ciceros in 0.001 cicero increments.

The computer allows you to mix the measuring systems, yet it is desirable to standardize paper size, typeface, column measure and vertical depth. Whatever system is preferable to you will be interpreted by the computer. However, changing measurement systems after beginning the layout of your design can give some rather garbled measurements. Some page-design programs allow you to set the document preferences for the vertical and horizontal measure separately; this will allow you to measure the column width in pica-ems, and the vertical depth in millimetres, if you so desire. There are 12 pts to the pica-em, which is a fixed measurement regardless of type size, and there are approximately 6 pica-ems to the inch. Changing the document preferences of the horizontal measure from millimetres to picas will allow precise control. For example, the indentation of paragraphs is normally based on a pica-em space of 12 pts. If you have set up the measurements in millimetres, to indent the paragraph one pica-

For further reading on the
use of typographic rules:

*The Chicago Manual of
Style*, 14th Edition (Chicago:
University of Chicago Press,
1993).

em, the metric measure is 4.233 mm.

To understand how the computer is calibrating between the different measurement systems, if your software has the facility, set the document preferences' points/inch to the default value of 72 pts (72 pts is approximately 1 inch). The dialog box would read 1p2.173 for a 5 mm indentation: just over 14 pts. The p is the number of pica-em spaces. Numbers after p are points, until 12 pts have been reached, which then becomes one additional pica-em. North American and United Kingdom typefaces continue to be measured in points and are normally referred to in point-size increments. The length of the line has been traditionally measured in pica-ems.

Deciding how many columns within the grid structure has a direct relationship to the size of the type and how many words can be used within a column. This is one aspect of the design process that has remained constant within digital design and human perception. How many words you use in a line will influence the readability of the magazine. Page-design programs measure the em space of the horizontal area taken up by two zeros (00), and half of this space, an en space one zero (0) of the type size being used. Printers have always regulated the ratio between typeface size and width of column to retain legibility. An example of size and length:

0000000000000000000000000000|00000000000000000000
0000000000000000000000000 | readability tolerance

abcdefghijklmnopqrstuvwxyzabcdefghij|klmnopqrstuvwxyzabcdefghijkl
abcdefghijklmnopqrstuvwxyzabcdefghij|klm

A column width should be no greater than 1 pt of type size to 2 em spaces of column width, and no less than 1 pt of type size to 1 em space of column width: approximately ten to twelve words. This amount of words gives a good line measurement for single-column text. However, when more columns are used together on the page this measure should be slightly reduced to eight to ten words per column, as both measures are within your guide-lines ratio. Too long a column measure and the eye can find it difficult to return to the next line; too short and the eye becomes fatigued

Although the rest of this chapter deals with typography, knowing line length and so on will influence your page-architecture decisions.

The column width should be no greater than 24 em spaces, or 48 zeros of the type size being used. The column width should be no less than 12 em spaces, or 24 zeros of the type size being used.

Another general formula for line length would be 1.5 to 2.5 alphabets. This also takes into account the 'unit of set' size for the typeface.

The space between the lines effects the overall greyness of the text. It also increases or decreases the readability according to how much space has been used. A long line of type will need more leading so that the reader can return their eye across the page to read the next line of text.

The space between the lines effects the overall greyness of the text. It also increases or decreases the readability according to how much space has been used. A long line of type will need more leading so that the reader can return their eye across the page to read the next line of text.

Correct line spacing aids the readability of the text.

Most default values are 20%; this is an averaged value for body text. You should reduce this amount of space for display sizes.

through spending time going from line-to-line. The third factor that can increase the line length is the spacing between the lines.

Depth of the Line

The typographic elements on the page can be perceived as contrasting through colour. Columns of text are considered for their greyness and headings for their blackness. Unused space is white space. Depending on the choice of typeface, and its apparent size, readability can be affected by the leading: the space between the lines of text. Originally, lead was inserted between the lines to increase the space. The characteristics of the typeface determined the size and variation of the body on which the characters sat. This gave the font an apparent size but not a true size. The space between lines of type could vary between typefaces. Computers measure the depth of the type from baseline-to-baseline (the words of this line sit on the baseline), and do not take into account the proximity of ascenders (dlkb) or descenders (pqjg) between the lines, unless optically-equalized leading (auto-leading) has been selected. Professional page-design programs then equalize the line space based on the amount of tall and deep characters on each line. Unlike the physical inclusion of lead spacing, computer software can equalize in fractions of a point measurement between the lines.

Type size, leading and the length of a line of type are inseparable. All three are highly controllable; like leading, the type size and column measure are capable of fractional point adjustments. Alter one of these three, and the possibility that the others have to be changed needs to be considered. A long line of type will need more leading so that the reader can return their eye across the page to read the next line. The leading for body type with between ten to twelve words in a line should be approximately 120% of the type size. Therefore, if the body size is 10 pt, then there should be an additional two points of leading. This ratio works well with body text. However, percentage spacing will look too plentiful when applied to display sizes. In sophisticated programs auto-leading characteristics can be set by percentage or by increments of .001 pt. The typographic attributes of the type family being used should also be considered.

The Apparent Size of the Line

Typography is an optical art and not an exact science. The relationship between font size, column width and baseline-to-baseline measurement can appear visually correct for some typefaces and awkward for others when a constant leading value has been assigned. It is the x height that optically determines the interlinear spacing: the greater the x height the greater the space. Although typefaces optically sit on the same baseline (the x height), ascenders and descenders can have different weights and sizes. The apparent size also has an impact upon legibility; the reader's eye will tire if the body size for a large amount of text appears smaller than 9 pt or larger than 14 pt. Photina has a tall x height, whereas Bembo has a smaller x height, making one appear larger than the other when they are both the same point size. The only way of knowing the true size of a typeface is by using the foundry specimen sheets for different sizes, or outputting your own for comparison.

The component parts of type that make up the personality of a typeface can be diverse between typefaces of the same point size. A magazine published in one typeface could well have a different number of pages than the same magazine published in another typeface. Characters vary in width for the same type size. For example, 11 pt Bembo regular has 51 characters, and 11 pt Photina regular has 49 characters, across a column measure of 20 picas. Both are *serif* typefaces. The computer needs to know set-widths (letter widths) and side-bearings (space each side of the letter). This determines how letters fit with each other. The computer does not measure the line of type in point sizes but divides the characters up into set postscript fractions. By measuring the line in units of set the computer can then calculate when the line is full and what adjustments need to be made for justification, hyphenation and so on. This allows the font to form other relationships with characters and spaces in the formation of words that have been pre-determined by the foundry. If the column measurement is short, avoid a typeface with a wide unit of set (wide letters).

Photina 12 pt
Bembo 12 pt
Photina 11 pt

The top two fonts are set in 12 pt. This is their apparent size. The font below is set in 11 pt. 12 pt Bembo appears roughly the same size as 11 pt Photina. It would, therefore, not be unusual to see Photina used with a smaller body size than Bembo for body text.

Counting 51 characters includes word spaces and assumes an average of 5 characters per word.

Reading from Line to Line

Ideally, the line length should be ten to twelve words so that the blink occurs at the line ending for the average fluency of a reader. The word space should be no less than the space occupied by an i and no greater than m of the font being used.

If white space is stronger on the vertical axis than the horizontal line of the leading, your eye will be forced down through the column.

Line space needs to be balanced with other visual considerations. For instance, justified type tends to create visual rivers running through the column if the number of letters and spaces in a line is less than fifty-one characters. If the line length is greater, then space between the lines needs to be considered. The eye will take the easiest return route to read the next line by following the line of white interlinear spacing. When the line has less than fifty-one characters, 'visual rivers' of white space flow erratically downwards through the column. Eye blinking tends to occur after reading an average line of text; these rivers encourage the eye to wander down the channel when the eye is refocusing during a line return. Ideally, the line length should be ten to twelve words so that the blink occurs at the line ending for the average fluency of a reader. The word space should be no less than the space occupied by an i and no greater than m of the font being used.

Digital type has no physical body for separation between the lines. Proper leading ensures that the tops and bottoms of characters do not touch. Too much space between the lines has the same effect: the lines become difficult to relate to each other. If you have a large volume of text and wish to alter the length of a publication, rather than increase the size of the type you could change the typeface, format of the grid or leading. These simple alterations should be considered at the beginning of the design process. Even after a satisfactory conclusion has been reached, no solution is perfect, and attention should be paid to the details. It is the optical balance between typeface, measure and space, and many other details that distinguishes the well-designed magazine page from the desktop published page.

IT'S ALL GONE PANTS

What do your knickers say about you and your relationship? We a...
three couples to show off their undies – with incredibly revealing res...

The easiest way to find out what a person is really like is to strip them down to their pants. Take the folks on *Big Brother*. From day one it was their pants that gave them away. Cocky Darren wore jockey shorts, both Tom and ... wore boxers to hide sudden, ahem, ... ments. As for the girls, flirty ... around in a G-string, and ... virginal, white knickers ... in pants can tell what ... also reveal what's ... onship? We asked ... other halves. Then ... ionship is ... Susan Quilliam ... bottoms up or pants down?

The top half of the page, all elements are contrasting creating a definite reading order. The bottom half of the page, elements are harmonious with no particular reading order..

Source: *NewWomen*
November 2000

Sarah Hopkinson, 24, and Hugh Medcalf, 22, both account executives, have been together for three years and live separately.

WHAT ... CHOSE

... got a drawer ... for my birthday. ... and he got my size ... I chose black ... sequins are trendy ... the bra will give me a ... Whenever I see Hugh, ... make a real effort.

Bra £16
Knickers £6
Dorothy Perkins

FOR HUGH: 'Hugh wears jockey shorts, which suit him. I hate tight-fitting shorts that show off a man's package – only strippers should wear them. I picked jockey shorts in small blue check for Hugh – they'll inject some colour into his pants as he always goes for plain styles.'

WHAT HUGH CHOSE

FOR HIMSELF: 'I've got four pairs of pants that I keep for going out and I'll always wear them if I'm meeting Sarah. I like plain colours and couldn't wear anything loud, although I own a pair of Wallace & Gromit pants. I chose navy Jockey shorts because I think blokes look better in simple pants.'

Jockey shorts £10
for two *Burtons*

... shorts £10
... Burtons

...OMS UP OR PANTS DOWN?

... **says:** It's very nice that they ... men should dress in the pants ... means they probably have

the same morals and attitudes. They seem to have an awareness of their fun streaks, which ensures this relationship is fresh and

Bra £12
Knickers £3.50
Dorothy Perkins

FOR SARAH: 'Sarah's got great taste in underwear, although she occasionally wears old knickers, which aren't sexy at all. I've chosen bright, pink underwear for her because she's got a great figure and I think they'd suit her. They're soft, silky and feel nice to touch. I don't like fussiness and frills.'

exciting. Sarah should take note that Ben values texture and is obviously turned on by what he feels as much as what he sees.'

Manipulating the Page

At the simplest level this can be described as:

1) The relationship of items to each other in the formation of one element.
2) Elements and their relationship to each other.
3) Establishing a consistent use for these elements.
4) Using contrasting elements to direct the reader.

There are four basic elements of design: headings, body text, images and white space. Each element can contain many items within, with the exception of white space. All page-design programs allow you to modify individual items within an element, or treat a group of items as one element. Colour is important, but it is not a basic element; any good design should also work well as black, grey and white. What is important to you is the ability to make the elements of your design merge or standout. This organization of elements helps to communicate your message more effectively. The organization of what is reproduced on a page takes place in your mind. This is the concept of Gestalt (German School of Psychology). Your perception of the world is always trying to form relationships; by understanding these relationships you can stimulate the reader and visually control your message.

The Relationship of Items in One Element

The basic building block of your design is the single item within an element. If you consider the number ten in a pack of playing cards as a series of ten individual square items, you very quickly perceive a pattern. These ten items can appear as two groups of five, or two lines of four and so on; your mind is trying to form relationships. If you then scatter the ten items, you randomize their relationships, the pattern becomes disjointed and the items lack any form. Items that are close and organized merge to form an element. There are no distinguishing features between the squares; they are merely items. If you understand this very basic rule of Gestalt, you can begin to organize the page. The simplest example on a page would be the characters that form a word or a symbol that brings together various items to construct one overall element. The logic of the process can then be followed through to

Your mind attempts to form patterns with the ten square items.

organize elements in relation to each other. When seen together with other elements, you will need to re-evaluate size, position and so on.

Elements and their Relationship to Each Other

As well as organizing shapes into patterns, your mind also stabilizes form and creates imaginary lines between elements by linking the line of least visual resistance. These visual connections are strongest on the horizontal and vertical axes. Your mind perceives a common line even though one does not physically exist, and so establishes a relationship. In the example of the number three playing card, there is a strong axial line which exists down the centre. At this point there are no distinguishing features between the elements; they are simply aligned.

Your mind tries to form relationships, but there is no pattern to follow.

The simplest example of page components would be words that form a line of type or paragraph. This will also be true of multiple columns of text hanging from a strong horizontal top margin. These elements have greater meaning because they are now working together in sequence. They harmonize with each other, but lack direction; other relationships need to be established. You need to prioritize these elements into a reading order for both text and image.

Using Elements Consistently

Three elements aligned on a vertical axis.

Your design needs to establish a regular rhythm to determine order. Your reader needs to be able to identify different types of information set within a hierarchy. Decisions need to be taken concerning all the elements on the page, such as the typeface for the body text, headings, sub-headings, captions and so on. This is also true of any illustrative material included within the design. In short, the establishment of a typographic style sheet that is appropriate to the design is needed, including a policy on the use of images. If you were totally consistent in your treatment of text and images, the design would lack interest; you need to alter the rhythm and retain a positive reading order.

Your eye is drawn to the bottom element.

If we continue to use the playing card analogy, you can now alter the size of one element and rank the reading order. The three elements at the same size have no definite starting point; they are

Your eye is drawn to the darker element first.

merely visually aligned. If you increase the size of the element at the bottom, your eye will prioritize that element, you are drawn by size. If you intensify the hue of one element amongst the ten, you are drawn by colour. If you alter a second square element to the same hue, your attention is halved, and so on. At the initial stages of your design, thumbnail sketches can very quickly establish this positive order.

Magazine designers regularly use these techniques. You are subconsciously directed around the page through their understanding of these principles. Open any high street magazine at an article, and note where your eye first falls. The established order for reading is normally accepted as top left, along, back and down one line to the next. By knowing this you can alter the reading order of the page, by altering the emphasis and position of the components. You can direct your reader to view a picture on the right-hand page first, and then to the top of the left page to read the heading of the article, and then allow their eye to begin reading the article directed by some other element used at the beginning of the main body of text. It is also an aid for the reader to very quickly decide if they wish to continue to read the article, drawing them gradually into the subject, layer by layer.

Basic Elements	Page Colour	Combinations of the 4 Elements
Headings	Page definition	**Conflict**
Body Text	such as blackness	No visual definition between the elements
Images	or level of	**Harmony**
White Space	greyness	Little definition with a close use of elements
		Contrast
		High definition with a positive difference
		between the elements

Contrast and harmony can also work together on a page. Contrast gives you a positive reading order, and harmony allows your reader to settle upon information of equal importance.

The four basic elements of design can be altered to make your page conflict, contrast or become harmonious. The blackness or greyness of the page can be determined through your choice of elements and how they are used. Contrast will give your elements a positive reading order. Major elements become primary information (everything you need to know about the article before you begin), and secondary information (the article itself).

Positive primary information such as sub-headings, headings, images and so on leave you in no doubt where your eye should go. Conflict should be avoided; most magazines demand a dignity that only a harmonious arrangement can provide.

The shapes that are not used create white space, and should also be considered as an element of design. When four squares are placed close together, a fifth white shape is created as negative space. Visual oscillation occurs when both positive and negative space is balanced. The reader is not directed or detracted from the elements. Add more space and the squares become four individual items; space serves to break up the relationships. These relationships apply equally to small items such as words and their letters, and larger elements. Columns of text, headings, and the position of the images all form these relationships with each other, and amongst themselves.

Magazines allow the reader to select subjects of interest very quickly. They use a relationship to achieve their primary purpose of communication.

Close together, the squares form a cross. When the space has been equalized visual oscillation occurs. The shape of the space has now changed and this can alter the relationship of the elements to each other.

Colour of the Page

Any good design should work well as black, white and grey. The colour of the page refers to the lightness and darkness of the page elements. Body text is judged by its differing levels of greyness. Headings, sub-headings and so on are considered for their blackness, and white space provides contrast between the two. The greyness of body text depends on the family, size, weight, line length, leading, justification or non-justification. By viewing the page as different densities of whiteness, greyness and blackness you can control the rhythm of the page, create contrast between the elements, emphasize the importance of certain elements and direct the reader around the page.

The colour of the page refers to the appearing blackness, greyness and whiteness of the page elements. Page colour helps to establish the reading order of the page. To see the colour of a page clearly, view it through your eyelashes.

White Space

Space can be considered at different levels; there is space between letters, words and lines. Blocks of grey text interplay with other elements of the design, and space between headings, sub-headings and images becomes important. These relationships are not finally resolved until all the elements have been brought together. Space

White space does not necessarily mean large blank areas of the page. Your use of white space determines how page elements relate to each other.

within a group of elements, such as at the beginning of a new section can allow the reader to rest or pause, look elsewhere and return without losing his/her place.

The reader should be able to identify which elements belong together. Too much white space within a group of elements creates visual holes in the design, and can disturb the reading order of the page. This is especially disturbing when the white space surrounding the elements is less than the space between the elements. More white space added to the outside of the grouping (left) brings the elements together, and can help your reader to focus attention. The squares on the previous page relate to each other, even after separation. When the page edges are added, these elements then form a relationship with the edges and lose their relationship with each other.

Headings and Sub-Headings

Sub-headings break the flow of the columns, create white space, and, like paragraph endings, can be a resting point for the reader's eye. Depending on the nature and extent of the text there is likely to be at least one hierarchical level of sub-heading importance. All categories of sub-head need to be considered in terms of how much differentiation is required. Sub-headings that overstate their importance can be distracting to the reader. Normally one or two points of larger type size with a stronger weight difference will be sufficient to draw the reader's attention without being understated. Typographically, the sub-heading should be a member of the body text family or compatible with the heading. Depending on the magazine, there should never normally be more than two contrasting type families within the design.

The sub-head break causes a change in greyness, creating contrast within the column. The reader can look away, and return with little effort. The space that surrounds the sub-head should be smaller between the proceeding text column to which it belongs. More space is desirable above, and will visually separate the sub-heading from the previous text. You can also run a sub-heading into the paragraph on the same line. It should be the same size as the body text, but distinguishable through a contrast of weight. Sub-headings also have the advantage of being added, disposed of, or edited, allowing the designer/editor another method of line control within the column.

A body text that reads well does so because of its blandness. These type families have normally been developed and digitized from old-style faces and have retained their elegance through the plainness of their form, such as Garamond or Baskerville. In magazines, headings can reflect more of the personality of the subject. The heading should contrast with the body-text size and draw the reader's immediate attention. The norm is to restrict typographic use to two contrasting families. You have full control over the direction of the reader; what matters is the contrast between the elements on the page.

You should avoid making headings and sub-headings all upper case, unless you are able to make letter-by-letter decisions regarding the shape of certain character-fits (how letters appear together). Upper and lower case has a better fit. Its overall density throughout the word means that letter spaces will require less adjustment. Any punctuation used on larger display sizes (headings) looks overly large and has traditionally been reduced by one point. Baseline-to-baseline measurements can also be less than the body text for display type. This adds to the blackness of the heading and increases contrast with the body text. There are many other combinations of weight and size difference that work well. Simply ensure that, on turning the page, your reader's eye is directed.

Upper case letters can have some awkward fits, such as the letter space between LA.

Text Alignment

Columns of text can either be justified, ranged-left, ranged-right, force justified or centred. Sliding type (arranged by your eye), which needs line-by-line optical balancing, is another option. Ranged-left text has a ragged right-hand margin. Justified columns of text have a flush left and right margin. Ranged-left and justified text are the most legible of formats, and are therefore probably the most common form of setting. Justified type suffers from irregular word spacing, especially over a short measure. Hyphenation can, in part, rectify this problem. For this reason H&Js (hyphenation and justification) are inseparable. Two consecutive hyphenated lines reduce legibility; three consecutive

The text alignment you choose will determine how many words can be used on a line.

You can decide whether words of a certain length should be hyphenated or not.

hyphenated lines can force the reader's eye to skip a line. Most page-design software allows you to decide how many characters are contained within a word before it is broken, and how many characters should be before and after the break. Your choice of column measurement and alignment will determine the frequency of breaks.

Ranged-left and justified text are the only practical alignment solutions for a column of text. Ranged-left text has even word spaces which gives a smoother greyness, and over a long column measure needs less hyphenation. The irregularity of the ragged margin also helps the column avoid static balance, appearing more dynamic than justified text. However, the ragged edge of the right-hand margin should be visually averaged. Any deep indentation into the column as a result of long words should be hyphenated. Unlike word processing software, page-design programs use an algorithm to hyphenate words. Again, the computer is making the value judgments, and some word breaks can be undesirable. Digital page make-up allows you to define hyphenation exceptions.

Sometimes, however, it is best for you to make the decision with a discretionary hyphen break. Most programs will also allow you to force the justification of a text line. This can solve problems within justified lines of type that require a manual hyphen ending. If large word spaces do occur, then change the tracking.

Ranged-right, centred and sliding type are not a legible option for the main body of the text. They should be reserved for typographic difference on the page, allowing the reader's eye to rest, and relieving the visual monotony of continuous text. Centred or sliding type can add emphasis to a 'pulled quote' (small block of enlarged text extracted from the article).

All these specifications should be added to the typographic style sheet, before the text and images of your design are imported into the document. This will ensure that work already undertaken in other documents will be combined as one, and no re-assignment of styles will be needed. This is because, in addition to creating new style palettes for the document, programs such as QuarkXPress will allow you to combine existing documents and assign one master style sheet.

Paragraphs

Even when the paragraphs have the desired endings, the way in which the reader proceeds from paragraph to paragraph needs to be considered. New text can begin by focusing the reader's attention to the starting point, using a graphic such as a symbol, drop cap, raised cap (large initial letter) and so on. Normally, each new text block will begin with no indentation (like this paragraph after a sub-heading).

After this initial start to the text, each paragraph needs to be clearly identified. Most articles tend to have a 1 pica em indent, with little or no additional spacing between the paragraphs. Additional spacing that does not conform to the baseline-to-baseline measurement will probably require vertical justification of the lines to ensure that the page measure is equal. This has the problem of making the text appear visually mis-aligned when it is set in several columns on a page. Additional space created by vertical justification and space between paragraphs that do not conform to the regular text spacing are less noticeable on single-column pages. For large single-column documents, page-design software is not the solution.

Normally each new text will begin simply with no indentation.

The next paragraph will need some form of separation, such as a 1 pica em indent.

Certain reprographic departments will reserve page-design programs for high-quality illustrated colour design, and use a system based on SGML (Standard Generalised Mark-up Language) for text-only documents.

Widows and Orphans

```
┌──────────────── Character Attributes ────────────────┐
│                                                       │
│  Font:   │SP Photina        │ ▼   ┌─Type Style──────  │
│                                   ⊠ Plain    ☐ Shadow │
│  Size:   │10 pt │ ▼                ☐ Bold     ☐ All Caps │
│  Colour: │■ Black ▼│                ☐ Italic   ☐ Small Caps │
│                                    ☐ Underline ☐ Superscript │
│  Shade:  │100% │ ▼                 ☐ Word U-line ☐ Subscript │
│                                    ☐ Strike Thru ☐ Superior │
│  Scale:  │Horizontal ▼│ 100%       ☐ Outline    │
│  Track Amount:    │-2 │                               │
│  Baseline Shift:  │0 pt │   ( Apply )  ( Cancel )  ( OK )  │
│                                                       │
└───────────────────────────────────────────────────────┘
```

Tracking a paragraph can remove widows and orphans. It can also alter the overall greyness of the text.

The beginnings and endings of paragraphs are an important detail. The typographic rules of your publication influence whether or not you increase the possibility of widows and orphans. A widow is a single word or a short line of text that falls at the end of a paragraph. An orphan is a single word or short line carried to the

A widow is all alone and goes on ahead. An orphan gets left behind.

top of a column at the end of a paragraph. The most common way to eliminate widows and orphans is to edit the copy. However, sometimes this might be impractical.

Depending on your column structure, it is possible to increase or decrease the tracking of the text. Over a certain depth of type the column will re-flow, eliminating the problem. A tracking value of one adjusts the character spacing by 1/200 em. Adjustment need only be +/–1 to achieve the desired effect. Tracking alters the overall character fit of the text and the overall visual greyness of the column. For body text, any tracking after +/–2 will make the overall greyness of the paragraph more noticeable.

Ligatures

Ligature character sets.

Ligatures are linked letters, either through their past association with earlier forms of script such as œ æ, or through visual considerations of how certain movable-type character-sets worked together, such as ffi ffl. Your eye reads the overall shape of the word, and by joining certain character-sets together the word shape suffers less disruption. Movable type created standards of character fit. Many special linked letters were cast as one with all the necessary visual alteration incorporated for that size of type. Digital type retains these special character sets. However, digital type allows both pair-kerned and tracked movement of characters. Because of this, justified lines tend not to require ligature substitution when the tracking is loose. Display sizes need a tighter fit and can create visually disturbing combinations if ligatures are not used.

Initial Paragraph Letters

Initial letters can fine-tune the reading order of the page.

Initial letters should be used sparingly. More than one on the same page reduces their impact, causing the readers eye to be pulled in different directions. Initial letters such as drop-caps, raised caps and hanging drop-caps on every paragraph disrupt the reading of continuous text. For drop-caps, most page-design software will allow you to specify lines of type depth for the initial letter. Line depth becomes disproportionate to the line length when five lines have been exceeded and lacking in impact at two lines deep. The leading value for the lines opposite the initial letter should also have fixed values to avoid vertical justification. Again, optical considerations affect the positioning of the letter; visual balancing might be required to adjust the apparent cap height against the top of the ascenders.

Raised initial caps should be at least twice the size of the body text and should sit on the baseline. Using raised initials within the main body of text causes spatial problems between the paragraphs. Like drop-caps, they should ideally be used at the beginnings of sections to direct the reader's eye to the starting point. Outdented hanging drop-caps (letters in the margin) need other special considerations. Like drop-caps, the top of the letter should visually align with the ascender line. With hanging drop-caps, letter shape is important, and they should appear flush right to the left-hand margin. Letters with a pronounced slant, such as W, visually drift away from the paragraph and should be used tighter to it.

If several initial letters are used on the same page with the same size and weight, the reader's attention will be divided by these competing elements. However, this might be desirable if the information is of equal importance (see the illustration on page 34). Instead of using initial letters, you can harmonize the page through the use of graphic elements. These can aid the reader by indicating the content of the information.

Colour

Colour effects us in different ways. Cultural factors influence the choice of colour, and your perception of mood and meaning. For example, in Belize, Central America, certain colours have stronger associations with political parties because of the general standards of literacy (election ballet papers contain colours to aid choice). Green is acceptable as a warning on hurricane posters, red is not.

Culture influences choice, and can sometimes appear irrational to those who have different values. There are however, certain objective factors that should be considered. For example, colour can create page harmony or tension depending on intensity or proximity. Contasting colours which are opposite to each other on the colour wheel (green and red) make each other appear more intensive. They resonate with each other. Harmonious colours are from the same half of the spectrum (yellow and orange) and are

Colour is mainly subjective, depending on culture. However, certain factors can be objective, regardless of culture.

For further reading see:

Phil Green, *Understanding digital colour* (Pittsburgh: Graphic Arts Technical Foundation, 1995).

Johannes Itten, *The art of color: the subjective experience and objective rationale of color*, translated by Ernst von Haagen (New York: Van Nostrand Reinhold, 1973).

more restful in their relationship. Then there is colour toning (tint) which is based on one colour with subtle variations through the percentage adjustment of the same colour.

Colour affects the overall contrast of the page, and what works well with different levels of greyness can be dramatically altered through the use of colour. Elements that balance in grey can become overpowering or understated when colour has been applied. When applying colour to any design, the alteration of contrast, the creation of conflict and reading order needs careful consideration. Page elements in the higher reading order such as headings, sub-headings, and so on, are your only real choice for colour applied to type, and will probably need adjusting in size and weight in relation to the tonal value of the colour.

Body text is meant for reading, and should be considered for its greyness against white paper. Colour reduces the legibility of body text when applied over a large volume of copy. If colour is to be applied to body text it should be used economically to draw the reader's attention to specific words or phrases, much in the same way as you would use other graphic elements or an initial letter at the beginning of a text. Like initial letters, colour should be used sparingly. Used once, will get the reader's attention, heighten impact, retain contrast and reduce conflict.

Colour on the Screen and in Print

True colours stored as RGB with 24 bits per pixel have 8 bits allocated to each channel. This gives 256 shades each: 16.7 million shades combined. CMYK uses a fourth black channel creating an additional 8 bits, or 32 bits per pixel.

Colour can be applied to different materials, such as buildings, vehicles, computer multimedia and so on. When a design scheme is applied to a building, interior and exterior lighting conditions will be different. Coloured material is adjusted according to the light reflected from its surface, helping the mind and eye to equalize colour for different lighting conditions and surfaces (metamerism). If the exterior and interior material were placed together under the same lighting conditions, they would appear to be different. Paper and computer screens both deliver colour to your mind and eye, and, as with other materials, they both need equalizing. This is achieved by colour matching and colour calibration through colour management. To understand this, you need to know how computers create colour and how paper reflects colour.

Addition: The computer screen mixes the primary additives, RGB (red, green and blue) light. These three channels mixed together create white light.

Subtraction: Two additive primaries combined create a third subtractive colour. If all three channels were mixed together they would produce black.

In full-colour continuous-tone printing, three subtractive colours, Cyan, Magenta and Yellow are mixed in various dot combinations to give the illusion of many continuous-tone colours. However, unlike mixing light, printing such densities of ink to obtain black would be detrimental to some parts of the image, and so a fourth black channel is added to make a four-colour printing process (CMYK). This process has a limited colour range (gamut). Most page-design programs have expanded the gamut by adding the Pantone Hexachrome six-colour process model. This goes beyond the four-colour process with the addition of vivid orange and green. Occasionally an additional special (spot) colour has to be included during the printing, because of certain reproduction limitations.

    When designing on screen, the computer is giving an interpretation of what the colour should be when printed on paper. Computers need a colour management system that ensures that the white point, and gamma response of the screen display, is adjusted to a colour-reference standard for paper. Any calibration of screen colours should reflect this difference. Most printers and designers use the Macintosh computer for print design because it has a built-in colour look-up table (CLUT). The Macintosh gamma hardware correction is set to ^1.4 with an output signal of ^1.8. PCs have no correction with an output signal of ^2.5. This means that images on a PC will print lighter than they appear on screen. The PC can have a graphics card installed to correct the problem.

CMYK depends upon regular half-tone dots to give an illusion of multiple colours. The dots achieve this illusion by using different size combinations. The dots for each colour process are set at optimized screen angles away from each other. If each screen were

Cyan, Magenta, Yellow and Black can be supplemented with vivid orange and green to increase the colour range. Hexachrome is a six-colour process ideal for digital colour printing.

not sufficiently angled from the others, when dots were printed they would create a moirÉ (unwanted interference pattern).

Hexachrome creates more screen angles. With a conventional dot structure there would be a definite pattern to the image. The solution is to use a randomized microdot structure. For example, randomization eliminates cross-hatching in skin tones and neutral colours, which contain the largest concentration of subtle colour blends. There is less detail loss and no moirÉ. A six-colour process is ideally suited to a digital press, because it is a dry process and has a tighter registration than an off-set litho press, and can reproduce the process more faithfully on subsequent reprints.

Hue, Saturation and Brightness: HSB is a further option available to you. Colour calibration becomes crucial if you want to use this model. HSB allows you to mix colour in the same way an artist mixes colour on a palette. Hue allows you to select a colour pigment, saturation adjusts the amount of pigment, and brightness controls the amount of black mixed into the hue and saturation. Spot colour models have swatches; three colour models such as HSB do not.

Spot Colours: Process-colour printing mixes the dots while being printed, to create the illusion of different colours. Spot colours are mixed before the printing process and applied to the press as a special colour. The mix of different inks depends on a reference number generated by the computer or as specified by you for that colour. The computer screen mixes light, a printer mixes ink. Spot-colour paper guides show the colour as it will print. If there is doubt between the two, a colour-matching paper guide such as Pantone, TruMatch or FocalTone should be used in preference to screen values. A printer will mix the ink according to the paper guide reference and not your screen.

The colour palette with rich black added.

Black is the only colour that overprints; other colours are made from translucent ink. However, black overprinted across certain colour combinations can still allow these background colours to blend with the black. This is when you need to use an additional rich black with the addition of 30% cyan, 30% magenta and 30% yellow. The combinations and percentages can be different.

Finally, the printing surface itself can be different. On coated surfaces the ink sits on the surface; on uncoated surfaces ink is absorbed into the paper. The same ink appears a different colour according to the surface. Sophisticated page-design programs have colour models that can emulate these differences for the same colour on screen. To help you distinguish between the two surfaces a suffix is added to the colour's identifying number. Coated paper has the suffix c, and uncoated paper the suffix u.

Images

Much of your design will need images to explain the points being made. Illustration has more power to convey complex ideas; photographs can be more decisive, their reality can better describe the moment. The way in which you initially plan the design will indicate the kind of images you require. Cropping parts of images and resizing can focus attention away from visual information within the picture that is irrelevant to the text. A well-composed image implies the mood of the text and further illustrates the story in the mind of the reader. To do this, an image needs to be imaginative, clear and focused on the main point.

Magazines tend to work within certain guidelines, according to the intended audience. Publishers will issue guidelines to photographers and illustrators alike. For example, publications that will be distributed in North America will require a different ethnic mix than Europe.

All elements on the page are considered for their relationship to each other, and image composition should be no different. Like other elements on the page, pictures should also avoid static balance. They can break the confines of any border, and create additional tension on the page.

The image can only aid the reader if it is visually concise in its message content, and is aesthetically pleasing. An image might not necessarily help if it is merely decorative, or when the text illustrates the story better than the picture. If this is the case, some other element to inform your reader, such as a pulled-quote, might be better. If the image is meant to help the reader visualize the story, it must also contain what is explicit within the text.

Clipping paths allow you to focus normal images.

Conventionally squared-up photographs should have white space flowing around them, with balanced space against the gutters and between the columns. Parts of photographs can be removed from their background and integrated with the text using

The focal point of any image is not necessarily the centre of the picture. Like other page elements, an asymmetrical quality is also desirable.

a clipping path (cut-out). Again, optical considerations are required. The text that runs around the image should not impede legibility by creating visual rivers through the type.

The reading order of any double-page spread does not necessarily need to begin with the heading; an image can be the focus of the page, and first in the viewing order. This order can be dramatically heightened by placing a large image on the right-hand page and text and small images on the left, especially if the other elements of the design are uncluttered. Visually heavy or large images are normally placed on this page for that reason. Magazines that have complex grids have more freedom of image use. If pages become predictable, the contrast of breaking the architecture using a cut-out, or bleeding off the page edges (5 mm of the image goes over the page edge and is trimmed off) enlivens the page and stimulates the reader. If the image fails to inspire because of the predictability of its content, then avoid using it. A bad image can destroy credibility.

The Digital Image

There are many kinds of imaging media, there are many ways to acquire an image, and there are many uses for images. Print demands a large amount of digital information if the required quality is to be attained. Images that are to be used only in conjunction with computer screens demand less information. Multimedia publishing opportunities allow files from the original source to be re-used in different sizes and formats.

Digitized images create many possibilities for different publishing media. You should consider different outcomes during the planning stage.

It is not only the appropriateness of an image that is important; there are also some technicalities that need to be considered. Images require a sound mid-tone range. They also require contrast with a good black and white at each end of the range. It is also important that the image is sharp, because reproducing the document in print sends the completed file through many processes. Each non-digital stage reduces the quality of what is being reproduced, and images with tonal values can suffer the most. The way in which an image has been digitized affects the final quality of the publication. High-quality print demands high-quality LIVE image acquisition by a drum scanner that has a full computer CMS (Colour Management System). Drum scanners carry

Each final file format for your images will have a different colour gamut (colour range).

out a range of tasks, including colour separation, sharpening the image, under-colour removal, grey-component replacement and so on.

DTP flatbed scanners import the digitized image directly into the computer, so colour management is only as good as the colour management of the imaging software, which in turn is influenced by the colour scanning depth of the flatbed scanner.

Algorithms built into the software to digitally interpret colour and density range determine the final output. The problem with PhotoCD as a LIVE image is not in the acquisition of colour, but in the limitations of the density range. This is most noticeable in the digitization of transparencies that contain sensitive visual information in the darker areas. However, Kodak state that, depending on the type of transparency film used, the final printing can be as good as any image acquired through a drum scanner if the image has been processed correctly.

The type of PhotoCD scanner dictates the kinds of transparency formats that can be handled. A high-end Kodak scanner will handle transparency formats other than 35 mm, and is capable of manually adjusting the image. However, this incurs cost and undermines the benefit of using PhotoCD. The finished PhotoCD will contain five file sizes for the same image. The largest file size for a 35 mm transparency is 2048 by 3072 pixels, which is adequate quality for a high-end output of a small to medium image. A Pro PhotoCD disc can contain an additional sixth file size of 4096 by 6144 pixels for a 35 mm transparency; the approximate uncompressed file size is 72 Mb.

Some page-design programs allow direct importing through a PhotoCD XTention or plug-in. For example, when you first install QuarkXPress, the Kodak Precision CMS is placed directly into your system folder as a start-up item. This is not the only CMS. Macintosh uses ColorSync and Windows uses ICM (Image Colour Matching).

The CCD (Charged Couple Device) of low-end flatbed scanners, and digital cameras that use compression for storage, should only be used for low-resolution output. Digital information brought into the computer needs to match the output. If the two are unequal either the file size is too big and space is merely wasted,

92 x 128

384 x 256

768 x 512

536 x 1024

3072 x 2048

Five PhotoCD file sizes.

More details of using PhotoCD can be found at http://www.kodak.com

If you manipulate your image, try not to lose data. JPEG (Joint Photographic Experts Group) in its extreme is a lossy compression. LZW (Lempel-Ziv/Welch) is a non-lossy compression algorithm.

For tonal images: the dpi should be twice the final lpi.

An example of low-resolution output would be: 144 dpi for 72 lpi.

An example of high-resolution output would be: 288 dpi for 144 lpi.

For line work: after 600dpi at a ratio of 1:1 no appreciable difference can be noticed for either high or low-resolution printing.

If a large line scan is to be reduced in the final document, make sure that fine lines have sufficient weight so that they will not degenerate when reproduced.

or the software tries mathematically to make up the difference when the maximum optical rating has been exceeded. The image becomes interpolated (adjacent pixels are averaged) to avoid pixelation of the final output; you are at the mercy of the software for the final result. This suggests that the best result will be obtained by the equalization of the dpi (dots per inch) and the lpi (lines per inch); unfortunately, in practice this is untrue. There is, however, a simple dpi/lpi equation between input and output for images with tonal values.

Line illustrations (no tonal values) should be scanned at a resolution to match the final output; there is, however, no appreciable difference after 600 dpi has been reached. If the line illustration is to be scaled after scanning, then problems will occur, and pixels start to become evident. Line illustration should be drawn to size and scanned at a 1:1 ratio or larger. The only other solution is to create the line illustration within a vector-based drawing program which retains the data to reconstruct the lines. Created as a computer file, the illustration can be scaled and sized accordingly, and then imported into the page-design program.

Designing on paper first will determine the required size of a digital image. These images can be cropped and scaled in other imaging software. Once the file has been opened within imaging software, the dpi information should not be reduced for ease of image manipulation; this causes interpolation when the dpi is recalculated against the final lpi for tonal images. When importing the image into the page design program you still have a small amount of upward-scaling latitude. However, any image that has been digitized should only be scaled downwards to avoid interpolation. If file size is a problem, high-end scanning produces an OPI thumbnail image for ease of manipulation, which will be replaced during high-end output.

EMINEM THE TRUTH

The power of typography is through the connotation that is associated with the characteristics of the letterform. Here the display typographic heading and the initial drop cap reflect the content of the article.

Source: *Bliss*
November 2000

He sings about incest, rape and murder and he's said to hate women, but what's rapper Eminem *really* like?

Hailie Jade Mathers looks up at her dad adoringly. Today's a very special day – her birthday – and she can't believe she's got so many lovely presents. "Is this one for me too, Daddy?" she gasps in astonishment.

This happy family scene isn't what you'd expect from Eminem, the 25-year-old rapper who controversially sings about incest, rape and murder. Especially when you hear that he once used Hailie's voice on an album track called '97 Bonnie And Clyde, about a man dumping a woman's body in front of their daughter. And definitely not when you realise that the woman he was talking about was his own wife and Hailie's mum, Kim.

"That song is a joke," says Eminem now. "Kim was trying to keep me from Hailie and this was to get back at her. It's better to say it on a record than to go out and do it."

Eminem's relationship with Kim has certainly been controversial. He's got a tattoo saying 'Kim Rot In Pieces' on his stomach, and although they only married earlier this year, he recently started divorce proceedings against her.

Understanding Type

The main type foundries all carry their family collections on CD. Monotype, Linotype and Adobe all allow you to preview their typographic collections. To unlock this material, you can purchase codes using your credit card. The Linotype Type Library CD has a wonderful little program that allows you set certain parameters such as gender and so on. The program then displays an appropriate type family. Typography is powerful because connotation is deeply embedded; we associate feelings towards certain typographical forms through images that are used in constant association with letterform in a range of media. If our choices do not take into consideration the connotation of the letterform, the message might confuse or give reason to doubt its validity. 'POLICE SLOW' does not work as an elegant script; it lacks authority if anything other than an upper case, *sans serif* in a bold weight is used.

This chapter does not classify families and their fonts for use on your desktop. Instead, it explains what to look for, and how to differentiate between the choice and variety that is available. There are many manuals solely devoted to showing a complete range of families. Typefaces are grouped into families, and changes in weight within the family (bold, italic and so on) are known as fonts. There are certain type families that continue to develop with each change in technology. Baruch Gorkin and Tom Carnase have researched a series of families from different foundries that have made the progression from metal through photo-typesetting to digitization. Their book gives a comparative analysis of the relevant factors such as outline, side-bearings, kerning and hinting (explained later) that influence typographical authenticity.

New technologies change type. Adobe's multiple master-fonts allow more control over letter shape, while programs such as

Baruch Gorkin and Tom Carnase, *The best in digital classic text fonts* (Graphis, 1995).

QuarkXPress allow you to split the outline path of individual letters, creating new typographic forms. Typography creates personality, and each typeface has its own characteristics. Typefaces are not intrinsically legible; you have learned their shape and meaning from experience. Any radical alterations that do not conform to what a reader expects reduce legibility. Type families and their fonts that you select for headings, sub-headings, body text and captions influence the way a reader reacts to your ideas. There are over ten thousand fonts that can be formed into more than two thousand type families that visually shout, whisper, demand and so on. These families can be classified into eight basic groups: Old Style, Transitional, Modern, Square *Serif, Sans Serif,* Decorative, Script and Gothic.

Old Style is influenced by the quill pen with lightly bracketed *serifs.*
Transitional represented a change from the quill pen to a more contrasting change of stroke.
Modern was the first purely typographic face with fine unbracketed *serifs* and a strong contrast between thick and thin strokes.
Square Serif moved typography towards heavy rectangular *serifs* with little difference between the overall letterform weight.
Sans Serif represented the functionality and versatility of the twentieth century. The terminal strokes had the *serifs* removed and there is little difference throughout the letterform.
Decoratives tend to be 'catchy' rather than legible, and are normally used for display purposes, mimicking computers, stencils and so on.
Scripts imitate handwriting, calligraphic, brush or copperplate.
Gothic fonts are more commonly known as black letter, such as Old English.

With so many combinations and possibilities at your disposal, choice can become subjective. Understanding design fundamentals, regardless of the technology that you use, will allow you to make objective choices. It is not the quantity of typefaces that you use that makes the design; it is your ability to recognize typography's

Linotype, *Linotype Collection: Typeface Handbook* (Cheltenham: Linotype Limited, 1989).

subtle differences. By doing this you can use typography effectively and in the right context. Adrian Frutiger explains slight typographic differences: 'You may ask why so many different typefaces. They all serve the same purpose but they express man's diversity. I once saw a list of Médocs all of the same year. All of them were wines but each was different from the others. It's the nuances that are important.' I always know when a student begins to acquire a typographical sense; when they complain that their preferred family is not available on the computer.

Choosing a Typeface

Until recently, small printers carried a limited range of fonts. Digital technology has extended the available choice to thousands. However, probably only fifty families form the basis of any good design. The characters within these typefaces fit well together within any word. For example, if you look at a line of type, the words of the lower case characters appear all the same size, yet physically the x sits on the baseline, while the c sits below the baseline and above the x height. Optically both appear on the same line (opposite). This is true of all well-designed *serif* and *sans serif* typefaces. A typeface that has been re-used over a long period tends to have a good typeface design.

The letterform of the Roman alphabet is an optical art and not an exact science based on mathematical positioning. Both the *serif* and *sans serif* can be traced back to the chiselled inscriptions found on Roman monuments such as the Trajan column. The characteristic of the *serif* can be attributed to the tools that inscribed the letters onto the stone. This combination gave the final inscription the shape of letters that we recognize, with stressed strokes of different thicknesses. Frederic Goudy was influenced by the letterform qualities of these inscriptions. By returning to source Goudy was able to use the past to inform typography in the future. All good typeface design looks back, placing this into an appropriate context for the present. Digital typography should be no different; it is merely another kind of reproduction.

Unlike the *serif* face, *sans serif* type normally has an equal monoline weight throughout, with squared features. Developed to

The x height is always given as a size value because it is the only character with four flat terminals at the end of the main letter strokes that rest exactly on the baseline and at the upper line of the lower case. The c is physically larger, yet optically equal.

McLean, Ruari, (ed), *Typographers on Type: An Illustrated Anthology from William Morris to the Present Day* (London: Lund Humphries, 1995).

express the aspiration of the twentieth century, it still converges on the past. For example, Edward Johnston's *sans serif* used for the London Underground in 1918 was based on the old-style script of the Roman inscriptions, the thick and thin strokes being given an even weight and the *serifs* removed. The face was an ideal adaption of the past for the London underground, where large single words needed to be clearly recognized against other competing styles of typography used in advertising. The design group Banks and Miles reviewed the design for the London Underground in 1979, adding new fonts to the original. *Sans serif* type families can themselves be sub-divided into 'uneven-width monolines' (Futura) and 'even-monolines' (Univers). The uneven-width retains old-style proportions, whereas the even-width monoline has modern-style proportions.

Sasoon, Rosemary, (ed), *Computers and Typography* (Oxford: Intellect, 1993).

Futura
Futura
Futura

Typeface Change

In order to understand these differences, it is important to look closely at the optical structure of a typeface, and the decisions around its construction. Newspapers, journals, traffic-sign systems and car manufacturers have produced their own versions. Monotype Times New Roman was developed for *The Times* and was probably one of the most successful typefaces of the twentieth century. If you consider the development of a typeface for a specific use, then Stanley Morisons' campaign for typographic reform in *The Times* serves as a good example. Before Morison, English newspapers where mostly set in modern faces. These faces tended to be of a fine typographic construction, reflecting the style that worked for a previous technology.

Futura is a *sans serif* uneven-width monoline that retains old-style proportions.

Printing-machine speeds and the volume of print were increasingly leaving the final newspaper impressions of these modern faces grey or squashed. Morison had made the connection and understood the problem of using type in the wrong technological context. His solution was to use modern features while retaining the legibility of an old-style face, and in doing so, regaining the clarity of impression that had been lost. The alteration of the typographic features of many typefaces such as Baskerville, Perpetua and Plantin were tested.

It was a revised Plantin that was finally used by Morison. The

The Times was set and published in Monotype Times New Roman on 3 October 1932.

re-designed family became Times New Roman, restoring both the aesthetic and legible qualities suitable for machine composition. Designing within a digital environment is no different, as Morison had to consider technical limitations such as ink-spread. PostScript fonts are outlines of the letterform, when printed there is hardly any distortion. However, when you use the fonts installed on the computer and you select Times, you are not selecting Monotype Times New Roman. You are probably selecting a different version. Each type foundry has a slight variation of their style for the same type family. Digital fonts are not physical; software generates the font as either an outline for the printer or as a bitmap for the screen. The font data is stored in the system and can be output directly to lithographic film/plate, inkjet printer or digital press, refreshing each character anew.

Typography has always adapted when media have changed. Digital typography has evolved to meet the demands of new technology. With movable type, each size had to be physically manufactured. Optical adjustments were made for the size differences of body text and display type. The creation of a digital version of a typeface is through informed interpretation; it is not a faithful copy of the original.

A more recent example of the use of digital type chosen or designed for an audience was when *MacUser* appeared on the shelves completely redesigned on 22 July 1994. Certain parts of the magazine went untouched. The *MacUser* logo was kept the same in order to retain the character and image of the magazine. It was the design of the magazine that changed and not the editorial contents; the same sections appeared in the same places throughout the magazine. This would have been done so as not to totally alienate regular readers. With the change a certain amount of familiarity had to be maintained. Like other high street magazines, *MacUser* has continued to change gradually through the influence of other magazines that compete for the same readership.

The senior art director and his team were aware that a large part of *MacUser's* readership were people who were involved in design themselves, and who produced magazines and other materials on computers. They were 're-designing to a critical audience, many of whom know as much as we do'. The three major areas of the re-design were in the structure of its format, and the visual elements and typography, but not the style or identity of the *MacUser* brand.

The new font families chosen for *MacUser* were Frutiger, Officina and Visage. Before the re-design, Franklin Gothic was used for headings, sub-headings and so on. Frutiger, like Franklin, has a wide range of fonts for headings, sub-headings and so on. Franklin Gothic appeared at the beginning of the twentieth century and went through a major revival in the 1950s when a wide range of weights were added to give the family versatility. Frutiger was adapted by Linotype in 1976, originally designed for Charles de Gaulle Airport, combining clear graphic communication with the aesthetics of good letterform. With their 'critical audience' in mind, *MacUser* carefully chose this typeface for primary use because: 'Frutiger Condensed can be used expressively, creating a limitless combination of possibilities for typography . . . The actual shape of Frutiger Condensed also provides the designer with opportunities for creative typography'.

Visage is a new serif font brought in by *MacUser* especially for the re-design, and it is used for the bulk of the body text. Based on an old style, the letterforms have a thick/thin transition and the contrast between both is relatively moderate. As the font is light in overall greyness, it is an ideal body text for reading. Officina, designed by Erik Spiekermann, is a *sans serif* monoweight with square *serif* overtones. A 1990s digital font, which is functional and informative, its overall greyness is darker than Visage. Officina links throughout the magazine, not only mixed with Visage for body text contrast, but also through the pagination and running heads.

What is important in the example of *MacUser* is that the publisher knows the profile of its readership and how it can attract an audience through the application of typographic design and editorial content. Each of the case studies featured later in this book strive to make sense of these points. For the students that wrote these case studies, there is an important lesson to be learned from analyzing any high street magazine. *MacUser* clearly shows that the re-design is specifically aimed at the readership, as it is

Display type Frutiger is used for headings, captions and so on, where the family's function is to inform and direct the reader's attention to the main body of text. Article sub-headings clearly contrast with the body text. They are larger and colour pushes them back into the page so that they are not overstated.

Body text Visage is a *serif* face used for the bulk of the body text. However, unlike a book, a magazine is not a continuous read. Officina is a *sans serif* used for smaller amounts of body text. It is mixed on the same page with Visage and Frutiger. There is sufficient contrast between the three to emphasize the difference.

perceived by the publisher. This profile is very important if it is to attract advertising revenue and, therefore, continue to publish. Since 1994, the re-designed *MacUser* has continued to evolve. Like other magazines, it is in a constant state of flux. Change becomes gradual or innovative, but always constant, and not alienating to its readership.

Like *MacUser,* anything that you design is aimed at your perception of the audience. Since the re-design described above, *MacUser* has moved on yet again to stay in tune with its audience. We all read magazines that interest us, and if you have back-copies of any title, the example of *MacUser* can be applied to it. If you can interpret the ways in which a magazine uses typographic design and why, then you are best equipped to adapt what you learn to your own magazine design.

Digital Type is Different

PostScript fonts comprise of the bitmapped screen information and the printer description. A font that has been digitized will draw the letter each time the character is called by the printer or by the screen preview. Each character has an optimum amount of plotting points to draw the outline of the letterform. Too many plotting points and the letterform's screen display and printing time are increased. Too few and the subtlety of shape is lost. PostScript has been developed for high-resolution printing and will appear in the font menu in different weights. TrueType appears in the font menu as a family name only, and its weight is altered using style descriptions. For example, PostScript Photina has additional 'expert' fonts.

To avoid printing problems during high-resolution imagesetter output, PostScript families should be used by selecting their appropriate font. Type styles applied to PostScript fonts will print on Laser proofs, but are ignored by high-resolution printers. When you print a TrueType font on a PostScript printer, substitution could occur if there is a font name conflict. The advantage of TrueType is that it has been designed for low-resolution Laser printers, giving the character more form at low-resolution. It also does not need a PostScript interpreter built into the printer.

Fonts tend to be designed for 'bottom-up' low-resolution

▲
HelveUltCompressed
Klang MT
L Futura Light
L Helvetica Light
LB Helvetica Black
LBI Helvetica Black O
LI Helvetica Light Ob
LO Futura LightObliqu
M Photina
Monaco
N Helvetica Narrow
New Berolina MT
New York
O Futura BookOblique
Old English Text MT
Palatino
Script MT Bold
✓ SP Photina
SP Photina Expert
SP Photina Expert Ita
SP Photina Expert Se
SP Photina Expert Se
SP Photina Italic
SP Photina SemiBold
SP Photina SemiBold
▼

The family highlighted is a TrueType version of Photina. The font ticked is a PostScript version of Photina. To change a PostScript font you must select a different weight from the menu such as Photina Expert Italic and so on. The PostScript family can also appear as a sub-menu.

output, or high-resolution 'top-down' output. Both give a false impression when used at the wrong resolution. The collateral approach of being neither for high-resolution or low-resolution output average quality at both resolutions. It is always best to know the final output resolution and choose accordingly. The Macintosh use of Postscript has mainly adopted the top-down approach for font usage. It is for this reason that PostScript top-down fonts can look badly constructed at low-resolutions. Characters can appear too tight or too loose within a word, giving a false impression of letter-fit, and of the actual thickness of the strokes.

The need to develop type families that take the guessing out of typography, and for use with low-resolution printing, is a welcome development. Indeed, the intention of the standard PostScript range installed on the computer was to give you a varied choice of display, body text, script, typewriter and computer-style typefaces. Taking the guesswork out of typography has seen the development of bottom-up fonts such as ITC Stone (International Typeface Corporation) which has a series of good weight variations and also a *serif* and *sans serif* version.

The low-resolution features ensure that the Stone family avoids fine strokes and joins associated with high-resolution printing. It has been designed for mixed use of the *serif* and *sans serif* without you having to consider how different families can contrast each other. Unfortunately, these low-resolution typefaces lack subtle differences, which becomes apparent when output through a high-resolution printer. To choose a family for DTP use, you will need to know what the final printing resolution will be.

In comparison, ITC Eras has been designed for a complete family use with no *serif* version. Unlike Stone, it is a top-down *sans serif* face that has a dramatic weight variation, from light through to ultra bold. The family also has a slight inward curving on all upright strokes. These variations are not detectable on low-resolution laser proof outputs, but are very apparent on the final high-resolution output. The family has no italic; all characters lean forward and the loops are not joined. It has a wide setting (wide letters) making the family readable as a text face used in small quantities and pleasing in display sizes. Eras is a recent uneven-

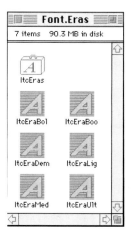

ITC Eras is a PostScript font. The top folder contains the screen information for the six fonts. The other files contain printer information for each font difference.

Ye Yo Yp Yq
Ye Yo Yp Yq

You read the overall shape of the word. Pairs of letters that have unusual fits can be pair kerned. This will reduce the space between certain letters so that the word appears together. *Bottom left.* Notice how the w fits under the crossbar of the T.

Bottom right. Tracking allows you to alter the overall spacing of the text. Larger display sizes will require greater tracking than body-text sizes.

width monoline designed by Albert Boton and introduced by ITC in 1976. Other top-down digital fonts based on older families can present problems of authenticity, especially when comparing the original font to the digitized version. Families that have been re-designed for use with computers have been optically compensated to incorporate new methods of reproduction. The design of digital type outlines produce what is essentially a new font.

Fitting Digital Letters Together

Computer monitors and printers work with pixels. A computer monitor normally has a resolution of 72 dpi, a high-resolution printer will have 2,540 dpi. The printed size of the pixel depends on the output resolution of the printer. What you see and what you get depends on the font outline plotted by the output device. Lower-resolution printers become less accurate because the plotting process is mathematical, and because fewer pixels to the inch decide whether a pixel is included or excluded during output. Well-designed fonts contain hinting instructions to reduce the arbitrary inclusion of pixels. Hinting attempts to retain the true typographical characteristics normally only apparent in high-resolution print.

Hinting attempts to faithfully reproduce the letterform, whereas side-bearing and kerning determine how letters fit with each other inside a word. Good kerning considers the overall

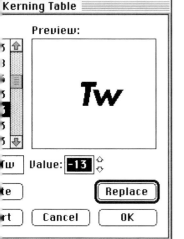

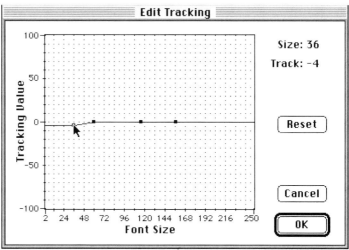

relationship of the pairs of letters. Badly spaced characters have a tendency to disrupt the reader. Side-bearings determine the relationship of space between a letterform and its neighbour on both sides. A well-designed font will set side-bearing values, which have an optical equivalent of give-and-take or wrenching. However, some pairs of characters require a special relationship; these character-sets are pair-kerned according to a table designed by the foundry. This table is alterable within page-design programs such as QuarkXPress. A font that has been designed with loose tracking side-bearing characteristics will require a smaller amount of kerned pairs. Fonts that have tight tracking and large pair-kerning tables contain more computer data, and will print and refresh on the screen slower.

Outline characters are mathematical. Points of letters are recorded so that the outline of the character can be rendered by the computer. Many points are required for curves. Curves on letters are not circular, and therefore require a varying curved line. To achieve this, curves pass through bézier points on the outline. Some page-design programs allow you to make shape alterations to characters. This requires a knowledge of the optical properties of letterform.

The Difference Between Body and Display Type

Body text is normally between 8 pt and 14 pt; display type is anything above 14 pt. Loosely tracked spatial relationships that work well on small sizes normally require tighter adjustment on larger sizes. True display type has finer strokes than body text. The optical appearance of display sizes needs to fit better because the eye is reading the overall shape of the word. All that is normally required of a body-text face is a plain, italic, bold and bold italic font for a complete family. Adobe has developed multiple sizing; these fonts contain the optical refinement of pre-digital fonts. A multiple will carry a small and large size where the font can be interpolated by size, weight, width and style.

The computer can also give additional variations to a font through the selection of a style such as underline, outline, shadow, small caps and so on. This is an averaged solution, added to the font by the DTP software of the computer. Linotype Times

An example of ~~strike thru~~ can be found on legal documents.

Cancelled is different from Times Strike Thru. You are at the mercy of the computer's software for the line width. Specially-drawn expert type variations contain additional character sets for small caps, ligatures, superior characters, old style non-aligning figures, fractions and so on.

If you are using a type family without an expert font set, professional page-design programs will allow you to alter the value for small cap font sizes, superscript, subscript and superior. When altering the horizontal or vertical scale of PostScript or TrueType fonts, mathematical and not optical corrections are made, and finer *serif* faces tend to suffer the most.

Tools, Type and Blends

The advent of DTP was originally associated with low-resolution 300 dpi output. Typographic democracy, but not typographic discrimination, was open to all. Early programs lacked the sophistication of professional publishing. Contemporary design using programs such as QuarkXPress now allows you to go beyond page layout, creating more opportunities than non-digital technology. For example, features allow you to alter the shape of letters and insert images as part of a letter or word's overall texture very quickly. Previous technologies could do this only through the skill of the designer. But even though the technology now allows you to do this instantaneously, consideration of image and letterform is still important. Characters with finer letter strokes can break up. Good word shape matters; after learning a word your reader recognizes its meaning through shape. The word as a readable image can have the meaning strengthened through the selection of a typeface that suggests subject association.

Harmonious and Contrasting Type

With DTP, mixing and matching typefaces is very easy. Knowing the reason why certain combinations work helps to clarify judgement. It is best to limit any selection to two families that contrast with each other. Two families from the same group used together lack adequate visual variation and conflict because neither are sufficiently different. Using one harmonious family for all typographic elements of the design maybe desirable if the magazine is intended to link throughout. However, if this is not the intention then contrasting family groups should be used: normally *serif* and *sans serif*.

There are exceptions; uneven monolines such as Optima are difficult to mix because the thick/thin transition of the strokes retains the characteristic of a *serif* although the *serifs* themselves have been removed. By knowing what to look for, and looking closely at the characteristics of the type family, choice becomes objective. The specific choice of family is then based on common sense and a concern for a balance between legibility and personality. The simplest example is a face such as Helvetica Round, where the *sans serif* is rounded and not square. In a heavy weight, this would be appropriate for fast food. Letterform creates meaning through association; the elegance of a script face would be inappropriate.

There are many *sans serif* families, such as Frutiger, Futura, Gill Sans, Helvetica, and so on. These straightforward typefaces aid the contrast of your design and are ideal for headings and sub-headings. For example, Univers is an even-width *sans serif* monoline designed by Adrian Frutiger for optical uniformity. Normally, a family of fonts is distinguished by being bold, italic, light and so on, but because of the range of weights, Frutiger dispensed with these descriptions and adopted a numbering system to indicate precisely where the fonts fitted within the family group. Lower numbers indicate light font variation, odd numbers are for regular, and even numbers are for italic.

Some page-design programs allow you to take display typography one stage further, by allowing you to alter the font outline and its fill. However, because a feature is there, it does not mean that it should be applied. To use this feature effectively the font needs certain characteristics. The simple shape of the heavier-weight *sans serif* families will survive such treatment, whereas a fine *serif* will not, as its features will compete for attention with the applied effect.

Headings, sub-headings and so on set the tone of the magazine's content. If your reader has reached the main body of the text, it means that they intend to read it. If you want people to read a long article, choose a bland face. Old-style *serif* families

Harmony creates a formal page when one type family is used with little variation between weight, size and so on.

Contrast emphasizes the difference between the typographic elements on the page.

Conflict occurs when similar type families with little or no visual difference are used together.

Sans serif makes a better display face for headings because of font variety and single-word legibility.

Serif faces are better for body text because they disrupt eye movement.

such as Baskerville, Caslon, Garamond, Bembo and so on look similar to each other and are all slightly irregular. This helps to stimulate eye movement. Stimulation through disruption helps to keep your reader alert, aiding legibility and making the blandness of families based on old styles ideal for large amounts of text. You can use a *sans serif* typeface for short blocks of text.

Research into the legibility of typefaces has indicated that *serif* characteristics enable readers to complete a text quicker. A family such as Bembo is one of the original old styles; digitization has produced a version with a distinct family range and an expert character set. What makes Bembo legible is the open counters and thicker *serifs*; like most *serif* typefaces, it has an easy letter-by-letter transition for your reader's eye. Finally, you must also remember that human perception changes and one clear method of dating your work is through your choice of typography. Typefaces that have been well-designed and continue to be used will ensure that your publication suffers less from ageing.

For further reading and examples of typographic trends and thinking:

Rick Poynor, *Typography Now: The Next Wave* (London: Booth-Clibborn Editions, 1991).

Publishing course at the
University of Plymouth,
Exeter campus.

Potential Problems

Documents that leave your desktop for output at another location must contain the page-design documents, LIVE images and all PostScript screen and printer fonts. Professional page-design programs will 'collect for output' by gathering all files and placing them in one folder, but in many cases not the fonts.

This chapter is mainly concerned with how your computer documents behave once they have been sent for high-resolution output. There are software solutions that will automate the process of checking what you send away from your desktop to be used by others or output at a high-resolution. For example, FlightCheck lists all problems and suggests remedies (more on this later). However, before simply installing software that takes the chance out of pre-press, it is important for you to know what the potential problems are.

Most bureaus will prefer you to send your files as documents, images and fonts. Others will except PostScript files, but cannot be held responsible for the final output, as this format has limited modification possibilities, and is generally considered uneditable. What you send is what you get back. The bureau will know the capabilities of their high-end equipment, allowing them to make alterations on your behalf that do not alter your design. Adobe Acrobat files are probably one of publishing's best kept secrets and are unlike saved PostScript files and EPS (Encapsulated PostScript) pages. Acrobat will allow the bureau to edit a document containing all the necessary layout, font and image data. If your design has more than one final output destination, Acrobat also has the advantage of making files visible within any WWW browser. However, simply collecting together all the files for output to a bureau is insufficient.

A beam of light moves back and forth across a photo-sensitive surface. The path of the beam is called a raster after the Latin for snake.

Desktop computing, including laser proof output, is an inexpensive investment; high-end imagesetter output through a RIP (Raster Image Processor) is not. A reprographic bureau is a service provider for many kinds of graphic output such as books, posters, and leaflets, as well as magazines. There is much to be gained from using the service provider correctly, and discussion of what you should submit for production as digital files, marked-up laser proofs and labelling of transport media should form part of your planning process. Knowing final image sizes and so forth is crucial for a smooth workflow.

The Scitex User Group UK has for many years been compiling reports from reprographic services that output computer files from different sources. Digital artwork is fluid, unlike artwork that was physically cut and pasted. Problems can arise when the files are transported from a Macintosh or PC computer to a high-resolution output service provider. When you digitally compile a document, the computer puts you in charge of the print production process. All of the decisions about how your documents are output, what problems the service provider might encounter and what costs could be incurred are taken by you. The Scitex UK document was developed as a discussion paper between publishers and reprographic houses. Most of this is based upon this document so that you can best understand what you are trying to achieve. 'Mutual and collective ownership of the project (from design through production printing) should be agreeably established'. This relationship is in the interest of both parties. If in doubt, ask; many bureaus will supply guidelines of their requirements.

LIVE Images

Laser proof and high-end imagesetter output is different; if correct digital output procedure is not followed then problems can arise. A well-planned project, planned in the same way as the design of the publication, will normally ensure that the computer document will require a minimum of processing. A LIVE image is any image element placed within a computer file that will be incorporated into the final output. This includes high-resolution scans and PhotoCD images digitized by somebody else, and computer scans and graphics generated by you. Before using LIVE images ensure that your Macintosh or PC has sufficient RAM to manipulate the images. If not, the reprographic service will scan images for you and retain the original for the final output. You will be provided with an OPI (Open Prepress Interface) thumbnail that you can manipulate with ease. The LIVE images will be replaced when the final document is returned for high-resolution imagesetter output.

These items must be marked LIVE on the laser proofs.

The reason for using LIVE images is to capture enough data to achieve the desired detail, keeping the file size as small as possible.

When you name a file, give it a name that has the same meaning for everybody (CaseStudy.tif instead of CS.tif). This will help memory recall later.

When using OPI images supplied by a reprographic service, do not rename the file. The file name is the link back to the high-resolution image stored by the bureau. It is best to provide meaningful file names for your images before they are scanned. Unfortunately, OPI thumbnails have limited graphic capabilities and can only be cropped and scaled, any manipulation within an imaging software program will have no effect on the stored image.

When requesting images from a service provider for manipulation it is important not to alter the resolution or CMYK colour model that has been provided. Using the algorithms to convert your file to RGB and then back to CMYK on your desktop computer can have a less predictable outcome on return for high-resolution output. Returning the file as a JPEG (Joint Photographic Experts Group) is a lossy compression; on decompression, pixels will have been down sampled (averaged against adjacent pixels) if the data is not present. If possible, always compress with non-lossy compression such as LZW (lempel-Ziv/Welch). Orientation of the original image is also important: pictures that have been rotated on your desktop computer will not have the algorithms to reposition pixels at a high-resolution. Rotating a LIVE image within a page design program could require the image to be re-scanned to maintain quality.

Lossy compression uses a technique that cannot expand the file back into its original data composition.

Non-lossy compression ensures that when the file is expanded it will be identical to the original.

Another option is to provide your own FPO (For Position Only) desktop scans. These must be clearly marked on the proofs, indicating the image that needs to be replaced by the high-resolution scan. The FPO must contain enough visual information to determine scaling percentage, position and crop details. When using a desktop scanner each image should be scanned separately, as opposed to ganged-up images (many images grouped together) scanned as one image file. This allows one single image to be placed into your computer document layout. Multiple images increase the file size, making laser-proof output slower. If you do decide to use multiple scans, crop each to size within an imaging program and save each one as a new file.

When scaling images, ensure that proportion is maintained between height and width (anamorphic scaling).

A problem with FPO files is that the service provider cannot reproduce accurately any graphic effects that you create with a low-resolution file. If the effects are simple or merely technical, make a note of the desired effect on the laser proof for the service provider to reproduce the desired results. If your desired effects cannot be achieved, an alternative would be to request the high-resolution image, and do any re-touching or special effects yourself.

When working with FPOs, certain characteristics must be taken into account: low-resolution PICT files usually look better on-screen than TIFFs, but worse than TIFFs when output to a laser printer. EPS files look good on-screen and default to the local printer values if the file has been pre-instructed to do so. LIVE and FPO images look exactly the same on-screen. This is because both appear the same at screen resolutions. Without clear instructions there is a danger that FPOs that remain within the document could be mistaken for LIVE files. It is always best to remove FPOs from your document before sending for final output. Make sure that the image has been printed on the final Laser proof which will accompany your layout document to the bureau.

Any image created within the computer should be treated differently to those that are scanned into the computer. Computer-generated images created within drawing programs call upon the necessary algorithms at the time of output. Therefore, the file should remain unaltered in the LIVE file folder and in its final printing position on screen. Image files have the greatest tendency to crash computers and hang laser printers. If this happens then it will probably happen on an imagesetter, as higher resolution output requires more complex processing. If your computer document does print on a laser printer, this does not guarantee that it will print flawlessly on an imagesetter.

If you are using a Macintosh with QuickTime, another option is to combine the screen and output qualities of TIFF and PICTS files. Save your Photoshop image as an EPS file with a JPEG preview. Unfortunately, the additional data required to render the image will slow the screen refresh.

Unlike TIFF files (Tag Image File Format), PICT files are intermediate files, requiring an additional format.

Using Fonts in a Document for High-Resolution Output

Fonts are probably the most widespread reason for interruptions to workflow. One of the most common faults occurs when moving the page-design document files from one computer to another. Fonts can be forgotten during transport, causing the output device to substitute an alternative like Courier. Another problem is TrueType styling applied to a PostScript font. Both PostScript and TrueType fonts will allow styles to be applied from the pull-down menu. Both will show typographic styling on-screen and on laser proofs, such as bold, italic and so on. When outputted, however,

Setting styles such as bold, italic and so on for a PostScript font creates a pseudo version of that family's font. Imagesetter RIPs ignore pseudo commands, and will print without the instruction in the font's original style.

PostScript fonts will remain unchanged, and default to the font's original regular style. Use the actual font variation for the PostScript family. The difference is obvious in the font menu. A TrueType font will only show the family name once in the menu, a PostScript family will show all fonts of that family that are available to you.

When a page-design document is moved to another computer, matching screen and printer fonts must be installed in the system or the document will not print properly. Version numbers and type foundry must be identical. Apple compounds the problem by installing TrueType fonts into the system folder, sometimes with the same name as the PostScript Type font. If an imagesetter has the PostScript font with the same name as the TrueType supplied by you, there is an additional problem in that the PostScript version will probably be used as the default by the output device, causing the document to re-flow. If you intend to use TrueType, inform the service provider. Most bureaus use PostScript as standard. Mixing both types of font within a document can cause problems, including longer processing times and sections of type being output as bitmaps.

PostScript and TrueType fonts are not interchangable. This is also true of different families from different foundries, as poorly written fonts could be node heavy (having been built with too many points), or have bad kerning pairs or incomplete character sets reducing printing and screen-refresh time. Fortunately, these characteristics tend to be restricted to display fonts that are normally used in larger point sizes and have limited use. It is best to convert such fonts to outlines; even well-considered fonts used sparingly at larger sizes should be converted to outline to reduce the printer font call. If the type has been used from within a program such as QuarkXPress, the 'Text to Box' command transforms the selected text into a Bézier-outline.

QuarkXPress will also allow you to edit the shape of the characters by selection of the Bézier points. If the type has been created outside QuarkXPress, such as type integrated into a logo or illustration, use 'Convert to Paths' in FreeHand, 'Convert to Outline' in Illustrator, and 'Convert to Curves' in Corel Draw before exporting to any page-design program. When text has been

---

Fonts	Pictures

Name
Bembo «Plain»

☒ **More Information**

PostScript Name: Bembo
File Name: Bembo
Type: Type1 Postscript
Version: 2

Check the font version in you page-layout application before sending for output.

converted it can be treated as a graphic and will not look for the printer font during output. However, any image imported into the drawing program and integrated with the type will be nested a further layer away from the page-design document. By importing images directly into your document in combination with type, any problems caused by losing parts of images will be reduced.

Foreign language fonts such as Hebrew or Japanese should also be mentioned because they usually require a keyboard file to operate correctly. If this file does not accompany the page-design document, characters will appear correctly on the screen of the service provider's computer, yet, like missing image files and printer fonts, will fail to print properly. The service provider will also require a keyboard map if any changes are to be made on your behalf, as the operator is unlikely to be familiar with the positions of the characters. PI (picture) fonts should be treated in a similar fashion, although a keyboard map is unnecessary for limited use. PI fonts are probably one of the most infrequently used fonts, but are probably the most overlooked part of any document sent to a reprographic house.

Like nesting (opposite), always use image importing. Never copy and paste images already placed in your document. Image import creates a route to the image file. This can eliminate high-resolution printing problems at a later stage.

Imported Files

Page-design documents treat imported image files as electronic pick-ups. When called for output, the document will follow the route back to the image file. After the file has been placed within the document do not move its location or change its name. This is why files and folders should be created as a digital 'job bag' during the planning stage. Documents look for the route, and so file names are a critical reference link. If you do alter the image file you should always update this in your document. Sophisticated page-design programs will display usage by showing the name, type of file and status. Most programs will allow you to see the path route to the file, the file size, when it was last modified and its dimensions.

Elements like these, that are designed in other programs for import into a document, can occasionally create other problems. An imported file sits outside the document (nested two layers deep) for purposes of printing. If, for example, a file has been created by imaging software and is imported into a drawing

File created in an imaging program (bitmap).

Text converted to paths within a drawing program (vector).

Image and converted text combined within the drawing program. When imported, the image is nested three layers deep, and the text is nested two layers deep from the printer. Import the image into your page-design application and use special effects.

program and then exported to a page-design program, the image file is now nested three layers deep. During processing the RIP will spend time trying to follow the links back. Nesting beyond two layers deep can occasionally cause problems; parts of the second layer will print, while the third could produce a bitmap or drop the image completely. The third-layer element can be isolated and placed within the page document and integrated with type, or saved as an EPS file for export which will retain the data from the third image, nesting both at two layers.

When your document is complete, unwanted digital data should be removed. It is insufficient to cover up unused elements with a white box, as the RIP of a high-end imagesetter will continue to process the data regardless. Return to the imaging program to crop any excess image area. Images that are cropped within a page-design document still process the data in the unseen area of the picture box. Images should be treated in the same way as film composition. The image should be digitized at a 1:1 ratio allowing 3 mm for each edge so that it can be fitted behind the edges of the picture box.

Trapping

Trapping is applying the lesser of two evils to resolve a problem created when some overlapping colours are printed. There are two major reasons for trapping: the movement of a printing press and the translucency of ink. Paper is normally white; when two translucent colours are over-printed a third colour is created. This is normally undesirable, except for black. Secondly, printing presses move quickly, and it is this movement that can cause mis-registration.

Mis-registration becomes apparent if one image (for example a square), had to be reproduced inside another larger square. The larger square would have a knockout (hole exposing the paper background) in the shape of the smaller square. The small square will fit inside the larger square, retaining its colour integrity. However, if the hole and the square were the same size, the movement of the press could make one square mis-register against the other. The result could be that two sides of the square could overprint onto the other square, and leave a gap on the other two sides. This would cause the white of the background to appear on the other two sides. To solve this, the smaller square is made larger, or the inner white background is made smaller.

This brings in the second factor: deciding whether the small square is made larger, or the inner white background is made smaller. Printing-ink colours are normally translucent, and whichever square is the lighter of the two colours will normally be increased in size. If the larger square with the knockout is lighter, the knockout is choked (the hole is reduced). If the small square that fits into the knockout is lighter, the ink is spread (the small square is made larger). The amount of trapping depends on the kind of press. The thickness of the trap value (the ink overlap) should be no greater than the press movement. You will need to know the kind of press and its amount of mis-registration if you intend to set your own values.

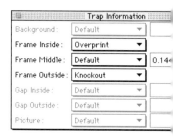

Fitting a slightly larger square into a smaller knockout will overcome registration problems. Size differences can be as little as 0.144 pt.

Small Type and Colour

Avoid designing the page with fine *serif* type that is less than 8/10 pt and which has been made with two or more colours. Like trapping, there is movement during printing, and fine small type printed using the four-colour process can mis-register. For the same reasons, avoid reversing out small type (the type is knocked out from the background colour to white) from screen tints built from more than one colour.

Single solid spot colours can also create problems for small *serif* typefaces. Spot colours are normally used over large areas because building a solid colour from several process colours can cause unevenness. Single colours mixed and then applied to the press can hold the amount of ink required to print an even colour. The amount of ink used to create the solid colour can fill in the *serifs*. Small *sans serif* type tends to suffer less from these problems because of the lack of fine character strokes.

Blends and Shade Stepping

Professional page-design programs allow you to apply a series of colour blends such as linear, rectangular, diamond, circular and so on. These can produce unpleasant bandings when tints do not smoothly blend into the next level. This can be minimized or prevented with a little more planning in the design process. There are several approaches to building a blend that will not band at high-resolution output.

While most page-design program algorithms for blends are sophisticated, if the combination of blends are apparent on a laser proof an imagesetter will improve the outcome, but the banding might still be evident. To reduce the possibility of banding happening when your document is output at high-resolution, increase the tonal percentage within the band range. A narrow range has a greater potential for banding. You can also visually disrupt banding by placing other elements, such as type, across the blend. There is also a distinct relationship between the length of a blend and the number of steps in a blend. Too few steps on a long blend will show banding.

Pre-Press Document Checks

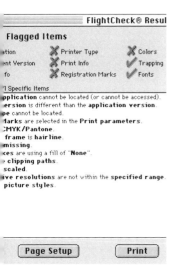

FlightCheck, Markzware.

Problems generally do not arise when you develop a document on a single workstation. Problems can arise when your document is opened on another workstation. The first part of this chapter has explained how your document images and fonts should be used. Proper planning of your document at the initial stage should reduce problems. Therefore, automatic checking of your document should be used as a fail-safe. The FlightCheck manual reminds you that 'one should always strive towards not using FlightCheck'.

Even the best-made plans are subject to human error. FlightCheck is a utility designed to analyze your document for an extensive range of problems. For example, RGB images that have escaped the conversion process are flagged, and colours that are neither Pantone nor process are brought to your attention. FlightCheck goes further and allows you to open images that have the wrong dpi output calibration and correct PostScript fonts which have pseudo style settings.

Digital Files Printed on a Digital Press

Digital printing brings the final output and your desktop closer together. It eliminates the preparation of film, plates and ink. Proofing becomes simpler because printing and proofing become one and the same. Digital printing also has other implications for the way printed material is distributed. Printing traditionally involves producing the publication and then distributing it. Digital technology changes this approach; you can distribute your magazine, and then print according to the actual demand. Wide-band digital communication networks enable your document to be distributed to different locations for output and/or customization to satisfy local needs.

Traditional printing works on the principle that grease and water do not mix. Full colour printing can only print on one side at a time because of the wetness of the paper. A digital press needs no water; ink for a digital press dries instantly so that two-sided full-colour printing is possible. With the digital method the sheet is fed back into the impression cylinder for immediate printing on the opposite side.

Another advantage of a dry system over a wet system is that the paper does not stretch, registration becomes tighter, trapping becomes finer and more colours can be printed easily. Some programs allow you to choose between CMYK four colour process and the Hexachrome colour process, so that you can send six colour process documents directly to a digital press.

Digital printing changes the nature of working, as the set-up procedure is simple compared to a conventional press. Your document is input directly to the RIP, which in turn makes the press ready. In the same way as you use your LaserWriter to proof the document, you can then print one or a thousand. There is also no wastage; colour registration is immediate, unlike a conventional press. Although digital technology allows you to output your document directly to film or to a lithographic plate, digital printing goes one stage further: directly to the press. Also, printing time is greatly reduced, and there is no reason why you cannot alter the document being printed so that each becomes unique. Imagine distributing a national magazine via ISDN to digital presses all around the country, each automatically customized with local features or listings.

Software that Leaves your Desktop

Fonts are normally the main software copied from your computer and sent to bureaus. Fonts come from many different manufacturers, and each has a licensing policy on how their software can be used. However, many type foundries have adopted the licensing policy of Adobe. While Adobe's license may influence other font manufacturers, questions about individual licensing issues should be addressed to that company.

Printers and service bureaus maintain licensed versions of all fonts used in their production process. It is your responsibility to maintain licensed versions of the fonts you use. Both you and the service provider should handle fonts in a legal manner, as licensed by each font developer. Fonts are software programs, and you accept that their license agreement usually states that the software should only be used on your computer. Illegal use of software reduces the research and development capabilities of the manufacturer. A weakened developer of software is not in your interest. However, because of the need to use bureau services to obtain high-resolution results, there has been much sharing of fonts.

Type foundries are not inflexible or unaware of practicalities, and, in recognition of this, Adobe modified their licensing agreement. Adobe fonts can be installed simultaneously on up to five computers by the same owner. Fonts bundled with other applications can only be licensed to a single computer. The fonts remain licensed for permanent download to only one printer. Adobe's policy on sending complete screen and printer fonts along with your document is that it is okay, as long as the service provider already has some licensed version of that type family. This is because different versions of the same font create different results when printing. By sending your version, the integrity of the document is maintained.

Licensing agreements change. This section is for your awareness and general guidance. You are legally bound by the current software usage agreement between you and the software provider. Check their current position.

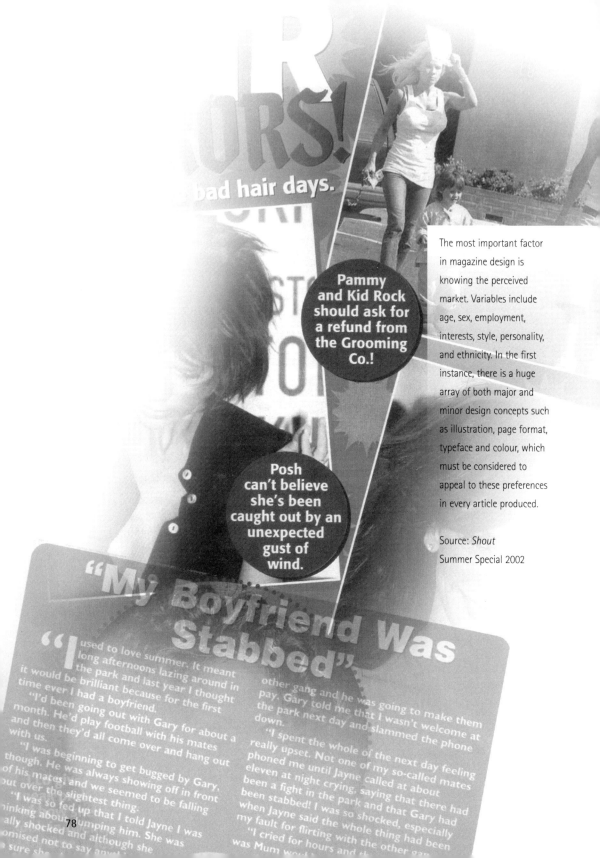

bad hair days.

Pammy and Kid Rock should ask for a refund from the Grooming Co.!

Posh can't believe she's been caught out by an unexpected gust of wind.

The most important factor in magazine design is knowing the perceived market. Variables include age, sex, employment, interests, style, personality, and ethnicity. In the first instance, there is a huge array of both major and minor design concepts such as illustration, page format, typeface and colour, which must be considered to appeal to these preferences in every article produced.

Source: *Shout*
Summer Special 2002

"My Boyfriend Was Stabbed"

"I used to love summer. It meant long afternoons lazing around in the park and last year I thought it would be brilliant because for the first time ever I had a boyfriend.

"I'd been going out with Gary for about a month. He'd play football with his mates and then they'd all come over and hang out with us.

"I was beginning to get bugged by Gary, though. He was always showing off in front of his mates, and we seemed to be falling out over the slightest thing.

"I was so fed up that I told Jayne I was thinking about dumping him. She was really shocked and although she promised not to say anyth... sure she... other gang and he was going to make them pay. Gary told me that I wasn't welcome at the park next day and slammed the phone down.

"I spent the whole of the next day feeling really upset. Not one of my so-called mates phoned me until Jayne called at about eleven at night crying, saying that there had been a fight in the park and that Gary had been stabbed! I was so shocked, especially when Jayne said the whole thing had been my fault for flirting with the other gang.

"I cried for hours and... was Mum w...

Essentials and Shout

by Jennifer Campbell

Magazines are not a recent innovation. In fact, they have been around since the early- to mid-nineteenth century, but at this time, due to their lengthy and laborious production, only the wealthy could afford them. In 1848, for example, a magazine could cost an ordinary labourer as much as half a day's pay. With the introduction of photography, firstly in halftones then later in full-colour lithography, both the time and cost of production dropped dramatically. As the new technologies developed, the design and layout of publications became increasingly complex and imaginative.

These days, the spread of desktop publishing and word processing software such as QuarkXpress, Photoshop, Freehand and Illustrator, coupled with the availability of numerous typefaces and low-cost inkjet and laser printing, have made readers more sensitive to effective design. When creating a format intended for public consumption, an essence of constraint is required by the designers. Ronald Walker reinforces this view: 'embellishment can often be helpful and appropriate, but its successful application is one of the most difficult aspects of page design to master.'

Ronald Walker, *Magazine Design: A Hands-On Guide* (London: Blueprint, 1992), p. 99.

The underlying concept of any publication is that it is still simply a means of imparting information; design skills should facilitate the process while creating a document which pleases the eye. The designer's primary role is to communicate and express content. Warford holds an even more stringent view: 'unless every part of the communication is designed to be within the recipient's understanding it becomes meaningless.'

H. S. Warford, *Design for Print Production* (London and New York: Focal Press, 1971), p. 13.

The suggestion is that design plays merely a supportive role to the conveyance of information, so should be subtle and minimal. This is perhaps the case in publications for which the text is of primary importance, such as newspapers or academic material.

However, a magazine should place at least equal stature upon its visual impact, since this is a major sales criterion.

The primary aim of commercial publishing is to produce a product to meet the needs of its target audience. Almost nowhere is this in evidence as much as in magazine publishing, where even the most narrow group of readers, classified by age, sex, hobbies and lifestyle, may still face an enormous choice of amenable publications.

In order for a single magazine to stand out from the rest, and offer a unique appeal to the discriminating reader, a great deal of consideration must be put into not only the editorial content, but increasingly to its design and overall appearance. A very different person will pick a magazine off the shelf with a picture of a car on its cover, to one preferring a fashion model, while yet another type will be drawn to a photo of a well-known celebrity.

As the potential customer flicks through the pages, they will respond subconsciously to every image that catches the eye: one person may be put off by long, unbroken chunks of text; another may be attracted images or colour; even a particular typeface may stand out as being slightly harder or easier to read than another. Then there are the subtler nuances: logos, advertisements, image placement and effects, bands and flashes of colour, all of which create interest and diversion to ultimately attract and seduce the customer into selecting this product above all others. Magazines are allowed liberties of design and rich visual appeal that would be overly extravagant in publications less dependent upon their appearance.

It is clear that the highest proportion of magazines are aimed at educated female readers, aged approximately between twenty and thirty-five. This makes competition amongst rival publications in this genre even more fierce, with many new titles continually emerging, of which only a handful will be a commercial success. The current leaders in the field are *Cosmopolitan, Marie Claire* and *Good Housekeeping*, with a combined circulation of over a million; however, the magazine chosen for this study is *Essentials*, which is aimed at a slightly older audience (twenty-five to forty-five) and covers a wide range of issues, including health, beauty, family, fashion, interviews and reports. In the accompanying media pack

Source: *Essentials*
September 2000

Essentials media pack
(September 2000), p. 4.

Essentials media pack
(September 2000), p. 2.

Source: *Essentials*
September 2002

1) Masthead typface has
stayed the same.
2) The dot has been
returned to the i.
3) The masthead now sits
within a solid special fifth
colour.

for this issue, *Essentials* claims a total circulation of 253,033, and a readership of 547,000.

Another core audience, not too far removed, is teenage girls, who might feasibly one day become *Essentials* readers. I have chosen *Shout,* aimed at ten to thirteen year-old girls, as a comparison to *Essentials.*

The most important factor in magazine design is knowing the perceived market. Variables include age, sex, employment, interests, style, personality, and ethnicity. In the first instance, there is a huge array of both major and minor design concepts such as illustration, page format, typeface and colour, which must be considered to appeal to these preferences in every article produced.

Having decided on all these factors, they must then be translated to a computer file and manipulated into the desired image for print. Other issues at this stage may include the practicalities of printing (colours used, cost, sizing and resolution, reproducing fonts), sourcing of images (original photos or artwork, cd files, slides or transparencies, copies of originals), sourcing of text (most commonly retrieved from a file) and application of style sheets, and the insertion of headings, pulled quotes, captions, folios, and running heads.

It is necessary to reverse and unravel these thought processes and considerations in order to fully comprehend the design skills applied to each of the selected publications.

Interviews in Essentials and Shout

Essentials treats interviews in a very traditional, informative way. The author recounts her meeting with the celebrity, combining passages of description, with a personal profile and snippets of relevant conservation, in around 2,000 words.

Shout gives the interview a 'questions and answers' format, offering no additional information beyond the celebrity's words. The article is only about 500 words long in total. Both magazines opt for a simple white background. *Shout,* however, adds a vibrant, brightly-coloured wavy border to the entire double page spread, patterned with stars of varying sizes. Both publications use full-colour photographs of the subject of the interview. In an

Essentials interview, the left page is given over to a full-page spread of Simon Shepherd in a casual seated position; the photo is bled off the page at the top, left and bottom, and runs slightly over onto the right page, before being cut off vertically. Other, smaller photos are used later in the article, but not within this double spread.

In a similar interview, *Shout* employs an entirely different technique: the main figure of Natalie Cassidy is cut out from its background and positioned slightly to the left of centre of the spread, bled off the bottom to show only the top half of her body. This treatment automatically establishes the figure as the main focal point of the spread. Five other much smaller cut-out views of the subject have also been used, each showing a different pose, with shadow applied beneath the feet, where visible. Four of these are positioned at the corners of the text, and one near the centre, providing additional foci.

Essentials has a very simple, four-column layout. Each column is 42 mm wide, separated by 5 mm gutters. The lower line of the heading and a pulled quote further down the page cause slight disruption to the text, particularly as it runs around the left part of the slightly off-centre quote. The only other elements are the running head and logo in the top right corner for reference, and the logo and folio in the bottom left.

Shout has a more complex format. The text is arranged slightly differently on each page to accommodate the figures. On the left, where the majority of the main image lies, two columns only, each 51 mm, have been used; while on the right a three-column format is seen, each 64 mm wide. A standard 5 mm gutter is also used. The main heading is printed over the corresponding image, as are the pulled quotes in the centre and two opposite remaining corners; the bulk of the text runs around the pictures. The blocks of text are also divided by both vertical and horizontal lines of stars.

There are no reference elements, as found in *Essentials*, namely a running head or folios. The primary objective appears to be to fill every available white space with some image, creating a very busy overall appearance, which is tiring to read and confusing at a first glance.

Essentials uses primarily a *serif* typeface (Americana Roman), in a bold, large and slightly smaller point size for its main heading, and approximately 10 point for body text. This is in fact not an optimum choice, as the weight of the type and very rounded lettering are not particularly comfortable to read in long sessions. A *sans serif* (Neue Helvetica Extended) is employed for all pulled quotes, and also for the introduction, which appears across the main photo on the left page; this combination of *serif/sans serif* fonts to disrupt the eye and provide contrast and interest, is common, and works well. An upper/lower case mix is also used throughout.

Shout, on the other hand, is neither restrained nor traditional in its font usage. The main heading uses an angled, heavy *sans serif* (Antique Olive Nord Italic) in two different point sizes, with a thin white stroke and also two grades of dropped shadow applied: a narrow, sharp, heavy one and a second broader and much fainter. The same font is used for pulled quotes, but in a smaller point size, with no stroke and only a single, heavy shadow.

The main text uses a contrasting *sans serif* (Gill Sans Extra Bold), possibly 12 point, but appearing very heavy and chunky due to the form of the font. The questions, which are bulleted, are all upper case, and slightly bolder than the answers. Although acceptable for small amounts of text, as in this case, such a heavy font would struggle over a more extensive spread.

The main *Essentials* text is black on white, but a pale green is also used to pick out part of the article heading, and to make the pulled quotes stand out further. A white type is also used for the introduction, which is printed over a dark part of the photo on the left page.

Conversely, *Shout* uses a very bold, gaudy colour scheme. Again, the main text is black, presumably for maximum contrast and ease of reading, but three other colours are used; the border is of bright yellow stars against a vibrant orange background; the same orange is used in the stars dividing the text blocks, half the main heading and all pulled quotes. Finally, a bright jade green completes the heading, and also the questions within the main text.

**PLUCK A DA
PULL OUT
ONE BY ONE
SAY THE OLD
LOVES ME; H
NOT'. SIT DO
A PATH OF D
SUMMER AFT
AND TAKE AD
OF PETAL PO
CHECK OUT A
IN YOUR ARE**

Shout's typopgraphy reflects the readership.

Conclusions

The target market is overwhelmingly evident in the elements comprising each magazine. The more mature *Essentials* reader has a longer concentration span and a higher interest in the actual written content of the interview. They are able to cope with the large text blocks with minimal disruption to the eye, therefore the style of writing, with passages of description as well as conversation, is highly appropriate. It is also easier to distinguish the article from surrounding pages, by the clear page numbering, indexed running head and distinct heading.

This publication is less likely to be read by the younger, professional *Cosmopolitan* type readers, as its style lacks elegance and sophistication. This is reflected in the types of articles and advertisements featured, which suggest a more domestic, practical reader, and the priority of cramming in a large amount of information in a fairly simple format. Its target audience is

My version of the *Shout* layout is not designed as a carbon copy of the original, but recreates the look and feel of the publication, making the content (extracted from *Essentials*) appeal to an alternative audience.

Essentials media pack
(September 2000), p. 2.

summarized in the media pack: 'Positive and vibrant women at a new lifestage; first home, child, husband! They have a lot going on in their lives and need a magazine which reflects this. *Essentials* inspires, guides and motivates, helping her make the most of all her life.'

Shout, on the other hand, is designed to seduce the much younger, fashion-conscious reader. The eye is immediately drawn to the bright colours and central figure, who would probably be instantly recognizable to this age group, allowing the heading to become less important. The text is designed for a much shorter concentration span, divided into questions with short replies, and broken up by the use of colours and particularly the lines of stars. Ronald Walker suggests that 'magazines for the very young and elderly should use larger point sizes than ages in between,' and this principle has been applied by using the very chunky version of the Gill Sans typeface. Combined with the large numbers of images, these factors all add up to expanding a small amount of information across a large spatial area, so that younger readers can quickly reach the end of the article without growing bored or becoming distracted.

Walker, *Magazine Design*,
p. 16.

The high use of imagery is also appealing to this age group, particularly in the use of cut-out figures and quirky postures to add and hold interest. This very gaudy look, using such bright, clashing colour, and with almost every available space filled, is confusing and unappealing to older readers, but conveys excitement and attractiveness to its intended young audience.

The significance of this study could be of enormous assistance in predicting the success or failure of a new or revised magazine format. Marcus Walters believes that 'if the design doesn't draw them in, chances are that nothing will.' It is also crucial to conduct extensive market research into both the target audience and competitors in the field. If circulation data cannot be obtained, it is possible to assess the success of current publications through other means. For example, a highly successful magazine will be able to sell a considerable amount of its premium viewing space (back cover, inside covers, right-hand full page spreads) to advertisers, and back issues should indicate both longevity and sensitivity to changes in the market.

Marcus Walters,
*Your Future in Magazines:
A Guide to Jobs in the
Magazine Industry*
(http://publishing.about.com
/arts/publishing/cs/
magazinelaunch/index.htm).

KERRANG!

www.kerrang.com

LIFE IS LOUD

AUGUST 03 2002/ £1.80

9 770262 662117   31>

DISTURBED RETUR

"STOP CALLING ME MAD
SHRIEKS 'MAD' DAVEY

GREEN DAY

THEY CAME, THEY SAW...
THEY BROUGHT A RABBIT

Bowling For Sou
Fat blokes get nake

I MISS JON. BIG TIME."

FEEDER

HE FIRST INTERVIEW.
HE WHOLE STORY.

OOF!

Source: *Kerrang!*
August 2002

Kerrang!

by Becky Gadd

Kerrang! magazine has long been established as one of the UK's leading rock music magazines, priding itself on its ability to know what the fans want. According to the editor, the aim is to cover 'a broad church of music. *Kerrang!* is a true bastion of positivism that tells it straight and speaks to its readers with the same fervour with which they buy music, gig tickets and T shirts.' *Kerrang!*'s distinctive look and logo have been in our newsagents since the early 1980s, but recent years have seen some intense competition for share of the weekly music magazine market, and this has prompted several rivals to alter their look with varying degrees of success. *Melody Maker* is one of the more famous names to have experimented with change this year: its change of format from a newspaper to a glossier magazine has perhaps been a contributing factor in its downfall. Their recent Christmas issue has just been announced as the last one ever, as its sixty year history comes to an end.

Kerrang! media pack (2000).

Re-design is obviously important in order to keep a publication looking fresh, but the problem lies within the amount of change that takes place and whether it affects the reader's sense of familiarity. This essay aims to closely analyze the design that *Kerrang!* has enjoyed for the last nineteen years, and compare it with the re-design which took place in November 2000. I will assess the magazine both in terms of how well the two designs show up in a technical light, as well as considering what the major changes are and whether or not early reactions to the new look are favourable or critical.

The Reasons Behind the Change

Unlike *Melody Maker*, *Kerrang!* is a magazine on the up and up: sales figures have increased steadily for more than a year now, and so the *Kerrang!* team decided to capitalize on this favourable position and made the move to re-design. Surprisingly, this was something that had never before been attempted in almost two decades of existence. According to *Kerrang!*'s designer, 'the attitude will be the same but it'll be much more "up to date" and less gumby-ish! Basically, the idea was to create a less dated look in order to please the current readership (the old *Kerrang!* logo, for example, was well and truly stuck in the 1980s), as well as trying to attract new readers. In September 2000, a brain-storming meeting was held where the core staff, internet people, and marketing people formulated lots of ideas about the re-design of both look and content. The basic brief was to update the magazine and make it appeal to new readers as well as the current readership.

Email from *Kerrang!*'s designer (5 December 2000).

Kerrang! has always relied on, and been proud of, its loyal fan-base, claiming that 83% of its readership buy every issue. As such, perhaps it has been possible to get away without re-designing for so long, because the majority of the readers appear to buy it for the content alone. However, it was felt that the time was right to lose the dated look and make the magazine something you would be proud to be seen with; something a bit more adult and less like a comic; something aspirational. In the words of the magazine's designer: 'We wanted to appeal to both the people that already buy *Kerrang!* but also to attract a wider audience, for instance, millions of people bought the Limp Bizkit album who don't buy *Kerrang!*, so we wanted to tap into that audience! In order to do so, the *Kerrang!* team looked to other magazines such as *Spin* and *Rolling Stone* for inspiration for new features, but also kept in mind the importance of retaining its USPs (unique selling points) so as to maintain the balance between newness and familiarity.

Circulation figures, *Kerrang!* media pack (2000).

Email from *Kerrang!*'s designer (3 January 2001).

An Analysis of Kerrang!'s Old Look

The overall impression of the old-style *Kerrang!* was that it was very eighties-looking, predominately due to the logo, but also to garish use of primary colours throughout the magazine. In addition to this, the type had a very heavy black look. By using a *sans serif* font for the body text, the weight had to be greater than if a *serif* had been used in order to make the text legible. Traditionally, *sans serif* fonts are regarded as being less easy on the eye, so using them for body text makes the process of reading long articles that bit more arduous for the reader. When you also take into account the dated fonts used for headings, and the liberal use of drop shadow, you can see exactly why the look of the magazine has aged so dramatically.

Grid Structure

Kerrang! uses a variety of grid formats, ranging from two to six columns per page. In order to give even greater flexibility, some of these grid structures are reversed on some pages, and in other cases, more than one grid structure is applied to a page. This provides variety, but also, at times, confusion. When the grid structure becomes too complex, it is not so easy for the reader's eye to navigate the page, and the whole point of the design is negated. A good design will provide the best reading experience possible, and should not even be noticed by the reader.

The majority of the opening sections of the magazine (including the contents, news, and gatecrasher sections) use a grid structure of three wide columns and one narrow one. This asymmetrical grid structure gives more flexibility of movement for elements and creates less static balance: it is both dynamic and stimulating. In this case, sometimes the grid is rotated and the narrow column is on the left rather than the right, for example. The basic design, however, remains consistent. Certain pages, though, are rendered more complex by applying additional grid structures. Good examples of this are on page four, where a five-column grid has been added, and page eight, where the grid has been reversed and applied over the original. This gives the option of having two narrow columns, one on either side, and provides more scope for the placement of images on a fairly graphics-intensive page. These opening sections are full of small articles, so each one needs to be differentiated from the others on the page. However, at times this leads to an overly busy page, and the hierarchy is in danger of becoming less clear than it should be.

As you move further into the magazine, beyond the news sections and into the features, the grid structures become less complex and easier on the eye. Some features stick to a very simple grid of three equal columns, and alternate with those articles which use a two-column or four-column grid. The simple grid design is necessary to let the reading flow for these longer articles, but other devices such as text boxes and images are employed to interrupt the eye at intervals and to keep the page interesting. Later on, some shorter articles (but nevertheless, ones which still form part of the main feature) use a grid structure of two wide columns and one narrow one. This particularly suits the format of a brief article with a fact-file in a text box alongside.

Things become more complex again in the various review sections of the magazine. Again, the design is born of necessity. Several short articles need separating on the page. However, this time the navigation is easier: there are certain consistencies of style which provide a feeling of uniformity. Effectively, they are all the same kind of article, a review; the difference is the subject. Hence, the only thing that really needs highlighting is the title (so that you only read the ones you are interested in) and the stand-first, which provides a synopsis of the article and a rating as to quality. Here, we have grids with anything from two to six equal-width columns, as well as a resumption of the three wide columns with one narrow one. Some of the more complex grid structures include one with six columns overlaid with four, three, and two.

Kerrang! Double-page spread.

Running Heads and Folios

All of the pages that feature a running head have the top margin denoted by a bold line. The running head sits on this with the top margin bisecting it lengthways. It is used to display an array of information. In the longer articles, it generally shows the author and the photographer responsible for the piece; but it is also used to continue the theme of a feature and reflect the heading on subsequent pages of the section in order to promote continuity and allow ease of navigation for the reader. The other use for running heads appears in the reviews section where it is used as a quick visual guide to the rating system for gig, record, games, and book reviews: not only does this provide a handy reference for the reader on each page of the review section, but it also eases navigation as it clearly delineates what is part of that section and what is not.

As with the running heads, the folios employ Frutiger as a reflection of the body copy. The folios do not appear on every page, but occur frequently enough so that the reader is reasonably aware of their whereabouts in the magazine. Each folio is in the form of a small rectangle (often in black or red) featuring the page number and the name of the magazine. This drops down from the line dictating where the bottom margin appears and bleeds off the bottom. Folios do not appear on pages where there are adverts or images at the bottom of the page.

Line Length

Line length varies greatly, according to which of the many grid structures is in place at the time. With a six-column grid, the character count is approximately twenty-seven characters per line. It would be even fewer than this, were the font size not reduced slightly for this format. There are jagged edges and hyphenation as a result, but the effect is lessened by the inclusion of inset photographs. There are few noticeable rivers of white space, due to the fact the articles are a series of very short sections with lots of sub-headings, providing less chance for them to show than there would be in standard continuous paragraphs of body text.

Some of the articles with wider columns (and therefore greater character counts) look quite bitty. Paragraphs are very short, so there are a lot of indentations and half-lines at the end of paragraphs to take into consideration. This could be improved either by justifying the body text (although this could create different problems in terms of awkward spacing and uneven page greyness), or simply making the paragraphs longer and leaving a line between each one.

Margins

The margin measurements of *Kerrang!* vary quite a lot throughout the magazine, sometimes by several millimetres, and do so according to the elements which make up each page. The margins are clearly delineated on many pages by a solid line. In the early sections of the magazine, all four margins are displayed on each page; the effect is to box in all the disparate elements and make them belong together in that section. In the feature articles, it is usually only the top and bottom margins which are shown, and this has the effect of uniting several consecutive pages, as well as providing a resting place for the head and foot furniture. There is a small amount of variety here in that sometimes the line does not extend across the entire page, and exists only to provide a basis for the running heads and folios. The only parts of the magazine entirely unaffected by these margins are advertisements.

Whilst the foredge and back margins tend to remain fairly constant at 10 mm apiece, there is a lot of variation in the measurements of the top and bottom margins. Sometimes the top margin is clearly greater in size than the bottom margin, and vice versa. In addition, they are sometimes equal at approximately 7 mm each. Obviously, this does not conform to the classical formula for the proportion of margins (2:3:4:6, with the smallest margin at 3 o'clock, moving anti-clockwise). However, the magazine does still endeavour to bear in mind that the visual centre of a page is further up than its mathematical centre, and employs other techniques to prevent it looking as if text is falling off the page. The use of images bleeding off at least one margin helps to balance the page and drag the text up. If a picture bleeds off the top, it balances the narrow margin at the bottom. If it bleeds off the bottom, it accentuates the space between the margin and the bottom of the page, and makes it appear greater. The text tends to conform to the grid, but visually the images are able to break through. Thus, they have the power to stimulate and interest the eye, but also to balance the page.

Typography

Kerrang! uses Champion, Compacta, Factory, and Saracen for headlines and sub-headings. Champion (originally developed for *Sports Illustrated*) and Compacta (developed by Fred Lambert in 1963), are both fonts developed precisely for the purpose of versatility. Champion is flexible because there are several different widths to choose from, and therefore there is no need to stretch the type. Compacta is designed for fitting headings into very limited space. It is a condensed typeface and was specifically designed for close letter and word spacing.

Factory is a font I believe may have been bought in especially by *Kerrang!*, as it appears to be unavailable from any of the websites and books I have consulted. Indeed, even *Kerrang!*'s current designer professes to know nothing of its origins. She suggested I look it up on the internet under Adobe Type, but even that yielded no further information. The font itself is quite pointy and jagged-looking, with slices chopped off the edges of letters. Although the look is quite distinctive, it looks extremely dated and very much shows its age. It is a welcome omission from the new design.

Saracen is a wedge *serif* font. It was originally developed as part of the Proteus project, as one of a collection of four type families designed in various nineteenth-century styles. The idea was that each family would be interchangeable, being of similar measurements and spacings. Saracen is not used in this way in *Kerrang!*, but the chunky triangular *serifs* make this font distinctive amongst the rest of the fonts used. It is used for headings, to highlight odd words in stand-firsts, and even for pulled quotes. When juxtaposed with the *sans serif* style of Frutiger, the contrast makes the highlighted words leap out of the page. However, its bold and heavy shape would be too overwhelming if used for more than a few words, so it is best kept for emphasising key words and phrases.

Frutiger, is used for all body text. Adrian Frutiger initially developed it in the late 1960s and its most famous use is on the signs at Charles de Gaulle airport near Paris. Its influence has now spread and its effectiveness as a typeface for signs has meant it is now used on the French autoroutes. Influenced by Helvetica, Univers, and Futura, the font is reasonably readable for body copy, but perhaps *Kerrang!* would be better served by using a *serif* typeface for even better legibility.

Body Text

The body text remains uniform throughout. Generally black is used, but if the background is dark, white is used. If there is any extra relevant information about the article (for example, when the featured band's next record is due for release), this appears at the end of the article in bold. This creates a heavy look, as the font has to be of a certain weight to be comfortably readable.

www.typography.com

www.myfonts.com

Headings

The headings all use one of the four fonts listed previously. This is perhaps the feature of the magazine that looks the most dated, after the logo. Red and black are used a lot, and drop shadow is used heavily as a device to make the headings stand out on some of the more crowded pages. For example, the news section and the gatecrasher section, both of which feature several different articles on a page, use drop shadow a lot. This is because the headings have to be smaller in order to fit onto such a busy page. They do not necessarily appear in a prominent place and so have to be distinguished and made to stand out from the body text.

Sub-Headings

There are more stand-firsts than sub-headings in *Kerrang!* The sub-headings that do exist, however, employ the same fonts as the headings, thus giving some idea of continuity. This also leads to contrast on the page (as opposed to conflict), as only two fonts (one for headings/sub-headings/stand-firsts, the other for body text) are generally used on a page.

Ranged-Left Type

All type is ranged-left, which works well some of the time, but can cause trouble if there are narrow columns to the page, where the effect is to leave a very jagged edge along the right-hand side of each column. This creates a scruffy look and causes a lot of unnecessary white space.

Pulled Quotes

Pulled quotes are done both in Saracen and Factory. Each has its own distinctive style: Saracen with its wedge *serifs* and Factory with slices cropped off the edges of the characters. Both share a sharp angular style, which draws the reader's attention immediately. In the main features, the pulled quotes are in Factory, and are often placed on the main image. This allows the page to make a statement of intent: by associating the two, it gives a brief, sharp visual and textual indication of what is to come in the article. Each quote has the person's name after it in bold upper-case Frutiger. This does not leap out so dramatically, but provides an extra point of reference if the reader is still uncertain about reading the article.

In contrast, the pulled quotes in the various review sections are taken from the reviewer, rather than an interviewee, hence, it is not necessary to include the name. The pulled quotes here are in white Saracen on a red box, and they are placed between columns, thereby making the text run around them. The articles here are reasonably short (too short to demand initial words) but long enough to need breaking up. The pulled quotes serve to visually disrupt, as well as to provide a clue as to the tone and verdict of each review.

Naked Lunch

When Bowling For Soup invite you around for dinner, it's hard to turn them down. And you don't have to worry about the dress code...

Words: Rae Alexandra Photos: Lisa Johnson

IF THE families living next door to Bowling For Soup frontman Jaret Von Erich had any idea exactly what he and his bandmates were up to inside on this sunny Wednesday afternoon, they'd put him under 24-hour Neighbourhood Watch surveillance. Jaret moved into the quiet idyllic suburb of Lewisville, Dallas just three months ago with his wife Melissa, and, for now, he's trying to convince those who live around him that he's just another ordinary guy.

But while he may have the house, a baby on the way and a cute pet Border Collie named Cappy, it doesn't take long to realise that Jaret probably doesn't share too much in common with his next to do neighbours. As he prepares for today's photo shoot, standing stark bollock naked, hands on hips, in the middle of his kitchen, he instructs his bandmates not to go outside 'au naturel' in case his neighbours see over the fence. And he's got a straight face. It's abundantly clear at this moment in time, that Jaret's having problems getting his work and his home life to get together smoothly.

"Yeah," he laughs. "This isn't a typical house. My wife's the bread winner around here for a start."

Kerrang! Heading, stand-first line and run-in capitals on the first paragraph.

Images

Kerrang! relies on a huge array of images, from the tiny little insets of album covers to full page pictures with the article printed on top, to some of the double-page spreads which often contain images that take up a more than a page. A mixture of black-and-white and colour photography is used, although even the colour shots contribute to the dark feel of the magazine because of their subject matter. Many of the photos are moody shots of bands or pictures taken at gigs, and this is reflected in how they appear on the page. The general pattern is to let the larger pictures bleed off at least one margin, making the page seem larger than it is.

Although the images used are largely photographs, *Kerrang!* does feature two regular cartoon strips: Pandora, which features in the gatecrasher section, and Continuum, which appears in the feedback section. Interestingly, although both are by the same cartoonist and take a similar format (full-colour strip running across the bottom of a page, not many frames), Continuum has been axed from the re-designed magazine.

Captions

The captions appear in italicized Frutiger, in white on a black background. Generally speaking, they appear at the bottom left-hand corner of the image. The title of the caption is done in upper case. The most noticeable exception to this rule is on the contents page, where the captions perform a slightly more important role and therefore must be that much more visible. Here, they use a different font (Factory) and tend to appear in a larger font size than the rest of the type on the page. Again, the title of the caption is in upper case, and the rest in lower. The captions appear in white with a thin black outline to them, and are not restricted to the bottom left-hand corner of the image, but instead are placed where they can best disrupt the eye's movement.

Stand-firsts

The stand-firsts are all fairly uniform, appearing to be in a larger, heavier form of Frutiger than the body text in order to stand out. Key phrases, such as any band names featured in the stand-first, are done in a different font (Saracen, a *serif* font) and in upper case, in order to visually disrupt the eye's progress down the page. This ensures that the reader immediately focuses upon who the article is about and can make a quick decision as to whether to pursue this article or move on to the next.

Initial Letters

Kerrang! does not emphasise initial letters, but initial words. These inevitably appear in different colours from the body text (which is generally black) and are done in a larger version of Frutiger, appearing larger still by being in upper case. This tool is used frequently to break up the text, particularly in the longer articles. An article which takes up half a page may use the device only twice, once at the beginning and once part way through, but the feature length articles tend to use it, on average, once in every column. It does not necessarily mean a change of subject or a new paragraph, rather it is used to make the reading experience easier for the reader: it prevents them from accidentally skipping text and gives the eye a brief rest.

White Space

Generally, the balance of white space throughout the magazine is reasonable. The elements of each page are fairly clearly defined. Perhaps the most glaring example of where it has been used badly is around some of the body text. Irrespective of column width, there is definitely a problem with jaggedness due to the type being rigorously ranged left. The way the paragraphs are styled (i.e. brief, no line gap between paragraphs, small indentation) means that there are a lot of incomplete lines, and more white space than there should be. This is exacerbated by the fact that the body text is quite heavy and provides stark contrast to the white space surrounding it.

Comparing Old with New

The re-design has not really brought forth many changes to *Kerrang!* The cover has changed fairly noticeably, as you would expect. As Jeremy Leslie comments in his book, 'the cover has to shout to the casual reader that this magazine is about x, while also addressing both casual and regular readers and explaining the content of that particular issue.' Aside from the new fonts used, the major alteration is the new logo, which not only looks a lot more up-to-date, but also conveys a more edgy, urban feel to the magazine. It also now incorporates the slogan 'Life is Loud!'.

Jeremy Leslie, *Issues: New Magazine Design* (London: Laurence King, 2000), p. 44.

The old logo is reminiscent of something you might get in a comic: the way the font has been designed to look as if a bullet has penetrated between the K and the E, the shock lines that resonate out through the rest of the logo, and the use of an exclamation mark, all contribute towards this effect. It evokes memories of the POW! and KER-BLAM! speech bubbles that used to appear in *Batman* and the like.

Old *Kerrang!* logo.

The new logo is a lot more subdued, although they have retained the exclamation mark, presumably seeing it as an integral part of the name. Instead of taking up the whole width of the top part of the page, and sometimes being partly hidden by the cover image as it used to be, the logo is now placed in the top left-hand corner and slightly at an angle, and nothing is allowed to interfere with it. Other changes include the incorporation of the slogan (which is entirely new) and the barcode, date, and price which have all been shifted from other parts of the front cover. Instead of the traditional pillar-box red for every issue, the colour used is different each week, and is selected to fit in with the general feel of the magazine. For example, it might reflect a colour which appears in the main image, or perhaps the cover page's headline.

New *Kerrang!* logo.

Frutiger is still used for all body text, although in a slightly lighter weight than previously. I think this is a major flaw of the re-design: the opportunity was there to reduce the overall greyness of the magazine (and therefore, its rather heavy feel) by changing the font to perhaps a *serif*. If this had been done, a light weight could have been used and the magazine would have become that much more readable. As it is, the greyness is reduced slightly by the better hierarchical structure of pages and the new fonts used for headings and so on, so the effect is not quite so disastrous as it was previously.

There have been wholesale changes with the title fonts: the new ones employed are Dax, Dirty, Blur, Dynamoe, Magda, and Coronet. The new title fonts are there to create a more up-to-date feel: they are more grown up and sophisticated than their predecessors.

Dax is prevalent throughout the magazine and features strongly in pulled quotes, stand-firsts, running heads, folios, and initial words, as well as headings. It is a *sans serif* font with a slightly rounded look. All characters featuring a curve are rounded at the top and bottom, as well as at the side. This font creates a pleasant feeling of being well-spaced: where it is used, there is balance and clarity to the page, in stark contrast with the old design.

Dirty and Blur were both designed by Neville Brody, one of the best known designers of recent years. He was, amongst other things, responsible for the advent of Designerism, the concept that if you create designs with a built-in obsolescence, designers will constantly be needed and will not go out of business. Dirty and www.fontfont.com Blur are both slightly similar-looking in that they both play with the width of individual characters and the spacing between them. Some letters are squashed close together, in contrast with others spaced wider apart than they should be. Narrow letters such as i, j, and f, are made wider, and this is particularly accentuated by Blur where the kerning varies wildly.

Dynamoe is a font that mimics the label-makers you used to be able to get, where a letter is pushed through a thin strip of plastic creating a raised letter in white. It has a slightly 3D effect: the characters are squareish and appear slightly raised. As it is a design indelibly linked with labelling, it is suitable to use as a heading with which to label articles.

Magda is perhaps most distinctively used in the introduction to the Marilyn Manson article on page twenty-nine. It has been adapted and made to look like an unreliable and inky typewriter's output, with some very faded letters and some quite blotchy ones. It also gives the appearance that not all the characters are sitting flat on the base-line or even have the same x-height, which lends a slightly amateurish, typed-at-home tone to the article. The initial words, and pulled quotes also use Magda, which enables the effect to be maintained throughout the article of several pages' duration.

Finally, Coronet is a fine, swirly, almost hand-written looking font. It is not used frequently in the magazine, but when it does appear, it is often used to contrast with another font. A notable example of this is in the heading 'Prince of Darkness' (page 12), where Coronet is used in conjunction with Dax, in order to convey the distinction between the two apparently different sides of the interviewee's character. Again, there is a statement of intent here: the heading attempts to create the tone and direction of the article through the wording and design of the heading. This is a strong example of typography as a form of identity rather than merely communication.

Although the *Kerrang!* team have made a point of hanging on to their USPs, such as the news section, the features, the gig guide, and the poster section, they have totally revamped some of these regular features as well as adding new ones, such as the crossword. Sections such as the contents page and the rising page (where up-and-coming new bands are featured) have changed their look dramatically.

Finally, the bright primary colours of old have been discarded in favour of more muted hues. This has been done to make the magazine look less dated. The new glossy cover adds to this more sophisticated appeal, and, although the quality of the paper is the same as it was previously, the overall impression created is of a magazine that has grown-up. According to *Kerrang!'s* designer: 'above all, we wanted to retain the same feel, that *Kerrang!* is the authority in loud music and that we won't sell out!'

Reader Reaction

Email from *Kerrang!'s* designer (3 January 2001).

It is a bit soon to tell, but what do the early responses tell us about the success of the re-design? In the 25 November issue of

Old content in new layout.

The two examples I chose to recreate in the new style were the contents page and the Rising feature, both of which have undergone the most noticeable change.

The contents page is a lot less cluttered than the old one.

the magazine, initial reader feedback appeared to be enthusiastic. 'I do like the new look . . . I'm sure that it will attract even more readers than ever', writes A of Lincoln in the letters section. 'I also want to thank you for the most devilish edition to date of your amazing, new-styled rock bible. I had to kick and scream to get myself a copy...' enthuses Nikki. Obviously, these letters have to be taken with a pinch of salt; after all, are *Kerrang!* really likely to publish any negative responses? But overall, the general consensus would appear to be good, and that *Kerrang!* have succeeded with

Kerrang!

(25 November 2000), p. 59.

their design. Ultimately, however, the true test will be in the sales figures over the coming months.

However, according to *Kerrang!*'s designer, there has already been an impact on sales even at this early stage: 'As for sales, they've gone up since the re-design and we are up 10% on last year. Our first issue sold around 50,000 copies.' So, although sales were already on the increase before the re-design, it would appear that the new look of *Kerrang!* has certainly at the very least retained its readership, and very possibly increased it.

The grid structure in the old magazine was a standard three-column one, which has now changed to two wide columns for the text and one narrow one to showcase the band's latest releases.

Conclusion

According to Ronald Walker: 'The prime function of page design is to get the copy read ... reject any design ideas which could confuse, fatigue, or in any way hinder the reader's progress.' In response to this, I would say that the old design of *Kerrang!* was fairly flawed and incredibly dated, and it was certainly ripe for re-design. I think the new design has indeed improved the look and the readability of the magazine quite noticeably, but feel that there is still more that could be done. The new logo and fonts are, by and large, a success, helping to create a design which looks much better balanced on the page. The chunky and spiky old fonts are gone, and this combined with the new, more subdued colour scheme, means that we are left with a more sophisticated look.

However, as I have already mentioned, I believe leaving Frutiger as the font for all body text to be a mistake, and would prefer to see it replaced with a subtle *serif* font. I think the main error has been to concentrate on changing page structure and headings fonts, whilst leaving body text largely untouched. If small measures were taken, such as justifying the text, creating a larger indentation at the start of paragraphs, and making paragraphs longer or leaving a line between each one, the overall look would be improved. I think the major changes have been successful. The new design genuinely does appear to provide a better reading experience than the old.

Email from *Kerrang!'s* designer (16 January 2001).

Ronald Walker, *Magazine Design: A Hands-On Guide* (London: Blueprint, 1992).

Hotline

by Daniel Carpenter

Hotline is a promotional magazine produced quarterly by John Brown Publishing for passengers on Virgin Trains. A mixture of entertainment and travel information, the magazine underwent a complete re-design for its autumn issue in September 2001.

The dual function of *Hotline* makes it an unusual design challenge. In an article in media journal *Campaign*, Matthew Cowen writes: 'the editorial mix covers so many bases that it struggles to persuade a passenger that it's worth trying out.' There is a tension between providing brand continuity and differentiating between the features and travel listings. According to *Hotline's* art director, 'it was time to update the image of this magazine and push it a little further within the very strict premise of it having to be associated with Virgin Trains . . . It must appeal to *all* passengers and must not be too cool and cutting edge . . . ' This tension raises issues concerning the relationship of design to editorial content that encourages a rethinking of the dynamics of design in all kinds of publishing.

The design of printed publications has, throughout history, been considered as being of secondary importance to the sense of the text. Even in magazines, which actively engage with design more than any other written medium, there is a very rigid belief that the quality of an article, when read with proper care and attention, is independent of what the article looks like on the printed page. The role of design, according to this principle, is to attract the attention of the desired reader in the first instance, and to ensure that the reader is not subsequently distracted. I would argue, however, that this deep-rooted underestimation of the role of design in the way magazines communicate ideas is not only misleading, but that it is part of a much wider misconception about writing, authorship and knowledge.

Matthew Cowen, 'Hotline: an expert's view', *Campaign* (7 September 2001), p. 10.

Email from art director of John Brown Publishing (27 November 2001).

Jan Tschichold and the Significance of Production

The main advocate of a more radical approach to the relationship between editorial content and design is the early twentieth-century German typographer, Jan Tschichold. In his handbook *The New Typography*, Tschichold takes issue with the modern use of old-fashioned design principles, which, once a necessity of the technologies of the scribe, are with modern technologies now arbitrary and not suited to the demands of the modern text. Reading practices change, and 'the speed with which the modern consumer of printing has to absorb it means that the form of printing must also adapt itself to the conditions of modern life. As a rule we no longer read quietly line by line, but glance quickly over the whole, and only if our interest is awakened do we study it in detail.' If this was not true in 1928, it most certainly is today.

Jan Tschichold, *The New Typography: a handbook for modern designers*, translated by Ruari McLean (Los Angeles: University of California Press, 1998), p. 64.

But apart from Tschichold's obvious practicality, what makes his manifesto truly radical is his formulation of the relationship between nature and technology. Whereas Western thought in the modern era has predominantly considered the two concepts to be antithetical, Tschichold emphasizes the similarities:

> Both nature and technology teach us that 'form' is not indepen-dent, but grows out of function (purpose), out of the materials used (organic or technical), and out of how they are used . . . In the process of giving form, both technology and nature use the same laws of economy, precision, minimum friction, and so on.

Tschichold, *New Typography*, p. 65.

Nature is conventionally understood as the source of all true meaning, with technology a contaminant, an interpreter of nature that, more often than not, bears a closer relation to the intervention of politics than it does to the truth of the text. Modern design supposedly detracts from the text; it is an afterthought, drawing attention away from true meaning. The only conceivable function of design is that of misrepresentation, and, quite frankly, it is best done without altogether.

And yet Tschichold breaks from popular conceptions to argue that the division of nature and technology is absurd. How can printed design be an unnecessary infringement on a text when it is a formal necessity of that text? It could not exist unless it had some design or other. The conventional layout of publications of the nineteenth century, despite (dis)appearing as natural and unquestionable, was nevertheless design. Indeed, it was because it was conventional, because the expectation of the reader rendered it transparent, that it appeared natural.

Tschichold's typography, like the theatre of Bertolt Brecht, demands that attention be focused back on the formal elements of production through *verfremdung* or making strange. For to realize that the text is indeed the product of the human hand and its contemporaneous tools is to deny it the authority of unquestionability, rendering it subject to criticism and change. Design is not incidental to knowledge, and unless it draws attention to itself, the regulation of knowledge is in danger of remaining in the realm of indisputability.

Page Hierarchy and Visual Prompts

Hotline is a perfect-bound magazine of eighty-two printed pages trimmed to slightly larger than A4 size (300 mm by 230 mm). It is divided into three sections: Frontline, Features and Destinations. The Frontline section includes news and entertainment, Features is for longer, journalistic articles, and Destinations (formerly Travel and Offers) provides information specific to train users.

The relationship between various elements on a page, including headings, text blocks, images and white space, is what produces interest and movement on the magazine page. According to Paul Honeywill, 'contrast will give your elements a positive reading order', as opposed to conflict between two completing elements which will give a page visual discord.

Source: Old *Hotline* Summer 2001

The Frontline section of both the old and the new design have different levels of contrast. In the old design, contrast is produced as a result of the difference between the size of the heading and body text, with sub-headings being set in a medium-sized font, allowing the eye to follow the page hierarchy in a logical manner. As well as logic, the effect of contrast in the Frontline pages of the old design is to create dynamism and avoid stasis in progression from element to element and page to page. This dynamic contrast is provided on these pages by page colour and images. For example, in a profile of Jenny Eclair on pages twelve and thirteen of the summer 2001 edition there is a very large picture in full colour taking up the whole of the recto page, in contrast to a very small picture on the left-hand side of the verso page in black and white. Additionally, there is white space on the verso page and the body text is set in quite a light typeface, giving the page colour an overall lightness, in contrast to the large picture on the recto page and the solid purple graphic. The graphic is a visual prompt, and is familiar to the reader as it introduces each Frontline section. Colour is also used to full advantage in the red headings; a very prominent colour that directs the reader through the page unproblematically.

Source: New *Hotline* cover
Autumn 2001

Contrast is used in the old design of *Hotline* both to keep the eye moving across the page (corresponding with the ethos of the magazine in its attempt to provide small amounts of exciting content reflecting many different tastes) and to direct the eye so reading is less of a haphazard process. In the newly designed Frontline section, however, there is far less visual contrast. The pictures used are more numerous and similar in size. The heading and body text are also closer in size than was the case in the previous design. The page colour does provide some contrast, as the body text used is very light, with narrow strokes, giving the text blocks a very pale grey colour. Along with the much greater use of white space in the new design, this contrasts with the pictures which are of good quality and intense hue. In spite of this though, it seems very much as if the designers of these pages have sacrificed the dynamism that comes from providing contrast on a page in favour of some other aesthetic principle. A new feature is the use of rounded boxes and curved lines moving between the various pictures and text boxes. This does provide a certain element of movement in the page, but there is very little hierarchy to guide the reader through in a logical manner. Visual prompts are not consistent either, with tiny captions and arrows introducing the subject of each block of text. It seems almost as if, in the new format, the designers of *Hotline* intend the reader to approach the magazine in an unconventional way. At the risk of making reading a very frustrating process, they have produced a design which encourages the reader to drift aimlessly from picture to text block, denying the need to attend to all of the content as it might have been meant to have been read. This puts the responsibility of reading back on the reader, showing how meaning is produced in the meeting of reader and the actual physical text.

Grids and Columns

Magazines usually have several grids which they use individually or in combination to structure different sections. In the old design of *Hotline* there are six recognizable grids in use, four symmetrical and two asymmetrical. Of the four symmetrical grids, two are two-column but have different gutter widths. The 10 mm version is used once in the Frontline section and the 4 mm version is used once in the Features section. In the Features section the more common grid structure is the symmetrical three-column grid, used in five of the seven articles. The Travel and Offers section invariably uses the unusual five-column grid. The two asymmetrical grids are used in the Frontline section, with the two wider columns used for the main body text and the narrower column used for supplementary text. The difference between the two asymmetrical grids is the distance between the main columns and the supplementary one: either 14 mm or 19 mm.

The old *Hotline* design does not overlap the six standard grids, giving only a limited degree of variation within the magazine. The effect of using an asymmetrical grid in the Frontline section of the magazine, however, increases the flexibility of the design. According to Paul Honeywill, giving columns of type an unbalanced axis 'causes visual disruption [and] is desirable'. Additionally, pictures and text blocks are often spread across the two main columns, producing an alternative wider column.

Although there is room for variation within the old design,

Recognizable grid structures in old . . .

. . . and new *Hotline* designs.

Hotline's new design has even greater flexibility, even though it uses only three distinctive grids. The three grids it uses are all symmetrical: the two-column and three-column (which are identical to those of the previous design guise) are used for articles in the Features section and occasionally occur in the Frontline section. The Destination section uses a six-column grid in place of the old five-column grid of Travel and Offers. As in the previous design, the new magazine does not appear to use combinations of layered grids; the flexibility of the new design, most apparent in the Frontline section, comes from a break from the conventional use of grids altogether.

The art director of *Hotline* told me that the new grid structure 'is actually quite loose and features are supposed to be visually more or less independent of each other due to the fact that they are also very different (sports, business, health, celebrity etc...)'. Whereas the Features and Destinations sections have a more formal grid structure similar to that of the old design, the Frontline section has a fluid structure with short blocks of text in various formations. The unifying elements in this section are typeface, colour and frames around text and image. In contrast to the other sections, Frontline is more content led; the nature of the text dictates its particular design. Articles in the Features section, on the other hand, are more template led; they have a regular two- or three-column grid structure, leading to greater restrictions on the type of content printed (for example, the text must be of a certain length, relate to a certain number of pictures, have a certain number of pull quotes, and so on). The Destinations section has the most rigid grid structure of all, with an almost identical template used for each separate destination.

In his *Campaign* article, Matthew Cowen's main concern about *Hotline* is the overtly train-related content of the Destinations section. His favourite section of the magazine is Frontline, which he describes as sharp and stimulating. This judgement, of course, is not only one of content, but of the design it is bound up with. A fluid design template, where every page is necessarily different, draws attention to itself as a product of the design process, giving a keener critical awareness of the way the text is addressing its reader.

Email from art director of John Brown Publishing (27 November 2001).

The new Frontline section has a fluid structure.

Lines: Length, Depth, Size and Alignment

The new Destinations section has a similar formal grid structure to the old design.

The various column structures used in both the old and newly designed *Hotline* mean that lines of type have various lengths, effecting the readability of each block of text. Paul Honeywill suggests that for a line of text to be legible it should be no shorter than 24 zeros of the size of type being used and no greater than 48 zeros. This approximates to a line of approximately ten to twelve words.

In the old *Hotline* design, the common grid structure in the Features section is the three-column grid, which on average has a line length of only seven words. This reduced line length corresponds to the use of three columns; if the lines were any longer then the type would have to be smaller to fit horizontally across the page, increasing the density of the text. This could be countered in turn by increasing the line depth, but the resulting text, with its small point-size and large amounts of leading would be fatiguing to the eye.

The new design of the Features section, which makes greater use of the two-column grid, has an average line length of thirteen words; the other extreme of readability. The danger of this is that it becomes difficult for the eye to return to the next line. The greater difference in line length between the Frontline section (which in both design guises has lines as short as six words), emphasizes the different ways each section positions its reader. Whereas in the previous design there was no great differentiation between the processes of reading each section of the magazine, in the new *Hotline* there is a great difference. The Frontline section, by using small blocks of text with short line length, encourages casual reading, while the Features section requires far more investment of attention on behalf of the reader. The design is explicit in the production of meaning; it is informing the reader that this is a more serious article and should be read accordingly.

The differences in the new *Hotline* encourage an appreciation of the way in which design is not neutral but instrumental in addressing the reader and producing meaning. However, the length of the line in the Features section does make it tiring to read for the length of time the article requires. In spite of considerations of how meaning is produced, it is of vital importance that a magazine must not alienate its reader to the point at which it loses its audience and ceases to be printed. The capitalist context in which magazines are produced means that they must necessarily be popular. This means that they must appear easily accessible; it is in their interest to play down the manner in which design 'interferes' with meaning. *Hotline*, though, is not conventionally commercial; it is not bought directly by the consumer, but is free to passengers on Virgin trains. Although of course, there is a commercial exchange involved, it is secondary and hidden behind a discourse of hospitality. As a result, *Hotline* is not so heavily policed by commercial factors as the high street glossies; it can afford to play around with the way in which it presents its information, producing designs which confound the reader and make them reconsider the act of reading. The *Hotline* designers have a much greater degree of potential creativity than those on other types of magazines. Whether making lines really long and difficult to read is the way to do this however, is doubtful.

Line depth, or leading, is not independent of the length of the line, and, as a rule, longer lines should have more leading to allow for the passage of the reader's eye from line to line. For an average line of ten to twelve words, the leading should be approximately 120% of the type size. The leading for both the old and new designs of the *Hotline* Features section, are around this value with 3.2 mm from baseline to baseline. The newly designed features, however, are set in a *serif* typeface, as opposed to the slab-*serif* typeface of the old design. The *serif* has a slightly smaller x height, making the columns of the new design slightly lighter in overall greyness, countering some of the effects of the overly long lines. Because the lines of the new design are so long (approximately seventy characters) the text can afford to be justified along both margins without forcing wide gaps between words to create 'rivers' of white that lead the eye vertically down the page rather than horizontally along the line. The lines of the old design were approximately forty characters long, and so the column is accordingly unjustified. Neither the old or newly designed *Hotline* uses hyphenation at the end of lines. In the old design this meant a ragged right edge to each column, while in the new design there is no similar effect as the length of line means the justification of lines of fewer words does not have as great an impact, because the extra space is shared between the large number of words in that line. The effect of having justified type in the new design is to make text blocks more like image boxes or graphics, with regular edges on all sides, drawing attention to the relationship between different elements of the page in visual (rather than purely annotative) terms.

Typeface

The right typeface is vital in producing a reading experience, be it an eye-catching one or one that is easier on the eye. Typefaces also, more than any other design element, provide a link to the history of printing and how technology influences our concept of normality.

The old design of *Hotline* uses a light *sans serif* typeface of the Gothic family (similar to the Linotype font Trade Gothic Light) for small or supplementary text blocks in the Features section and for most of the Travel and Offers section, corresponding to the shortness of the text. *Serif* typefaces are generally considered to be easier to read in long sections of text as they provide better definition for each letter and word-form. The main body typeface, used in both the Frontline and Features section, as well as sub-headings and pull-quotes is an unusual semi-*serif* type characterised by single slab-*serifs* on the left-hand side of the tops of letters and the bottom right-hand side of the letters a and d only. The only other typeface used in the old design is that of the masthead, which also constitutes the folio at the bottom of each page. This appears to be a bold version of the Linotype font Clarendon black, although with a slight variation (the negative space inside the letter o has, in the masthead, parallel sides).

The new *Hotline* design uses the same *sans serif* typeface from the Gothic family in the Frontline and Destinations sections. The major change in the new design, however, is the new body typeface for the Features section. Returning to a more traditional *serif* font (none of which were used in the previous design at all), the new typeface better suits the extended length of line in this section, easing what is potentially a very tiresome large block of text. The new typeface, although with undoubted features of traditional *serifs* (tapering at the top left-hand side of ascenders and the bottom right-hand side of the letters a and d) and a varying stroke thickness, also has aspects of the slab-*serif*, with block-shaped *serifs* at the ends of many of the other strokes. Two enlarged letters of this font are used as a graphic at the beginning of an article on Stella McCartney on page thirty-one of the autumn issue. With the prominent vertical *serifs* on the letter S and the varying widths of the two diagonal strokes of the letter M, this typeface has much in common with the Linotype fonts Candida and Joanna. The tapering *serifs*, alternatively, have more in common with some of the Modern Linotype faces.

Neither old nor new designs provide a great contrast in typeface, as those used in each section are very similar in both display and body text. Paul Honeywill notes that for a page to remain harmonious, 'it is best to limit any selection to two families that contrast with each other'. Although each magazine is limited to not more than two families (*sans serif* and slab- or semi-*serif*) each page rarely has both working in contrast. The effect of this, especially in the new design, which in its cover feature uses the same type for its graphic, heading and body text, is to diffuse attention and negate the page's potential dynamism.

Standardization and Flexibility in Hotline

The most striking change in the new *Hotline* is the masthead. The original masthead was set in a bold slab-*serif* type, whereas the new one is a slightly redrawn version of the Fontfont typeface DIN Mittelschrift. The new masthead appears more economical and understated, better reflecting the trend towards functionality over decoration of early twenty-first century design. The increasing use of *sans serif* typefaces throughout the magazine, combined with the tendency to present information in small blocks (especially in the Frontline section of the magazine) also reflects the influence of digital design on printed publications. Reading the magazine has become more like accessing a website, with *sans serif* type the on-screen norm and small lexias the foundation of hypertext.

The DIN typeface of the new *Hotline* masthead was adopted in Tschichold's era by the *Deutsche Industrie-Normen*, an institution

HotLine

The old *Hotline* masthead, with bold slab-*serifs*.

HOTLINE

The new *Hotline* masthead; more economical and understated.

based on the need for standardization in German industry. DIN first implemented the format of paper sizes used today, including A4 size, the format on which *Hotline* is based. However, the fact that *Hotline* uses a redrawn version of the typeface (with the middle horizontal of the E extended), and is 20 mm wider than the standard A4 size, is almost an insult to standardization, the *raison d'être* of DIN. Tschichold was a strong supporter of standardization, believing that given a recognized and accepted framework the designer could allow the text to resolve itself, producing an organic and effective design. Standardization is where a radical reading of Tschichold's typography becomes more difficult, for if new conventions are implemented and become standard, soon the formal aspect of texts will again become familiar and divorced from the meaning of the text as it exists at that particular point in history. *The New Typography* is very much an arena of conflict between forces of popularism and the denial of individuality, representing the political pressures in Europe at that time, and presenting texts that embody ambiguous politics.

Hotline, and similar contemporary magazines, in employing a loose approach to typographic design are actually promoting more radical readings than they would if they were governed by strict standards. If all the sections of a magazine were alike then the concept of an intended readership for which the design was specifically formulated would become redundant. As a result, there would not be a space for critics like *Campaign*'s Matthew Cowen to assess the appropriateness of *Hotline's* content for that same intended reader.

The new design guise of *Hotline* has greater fluidity and a more relaxed relation to standards than the previous format, making better use of the greater flexibility of digital technologies. However, it does not exist in isolation and constantly bears witness to important patterns in the history of design. All magazines function somewhere in the gap between what has gone before and the possibilities opened up by digital design and the opportunity to target new groups of readers. What *Hotline* does, by using a flexible format to avoid the dominance of the editorial over visual content, is to make its position explicit and encourage debate on the significance of design.

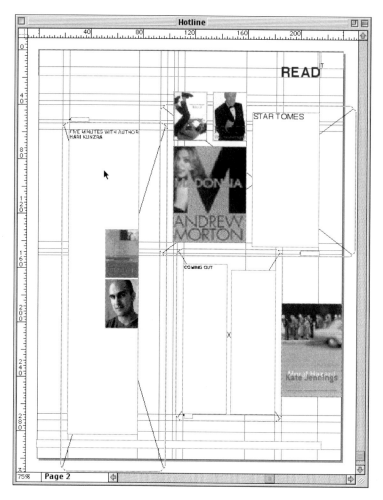

Using text and pictures scanned from another magazine, I have used QuarkXPress to produce a book reviews page in the style of the Frontline section of both the old and the new design. The new Frontline design version is reproduced here.

The older design supported longer text blocks, as there was less white space on the page. The new design, however, relies on smaller blocks of text separated by more obvious design elements such as rounded boxes, overlap and white space.

Conclusion

In the course of this investigation I have tried to demonstrate that design does not exist independently of the culture and specifics of its production. To think of design as divorced from the designer is to render certain types of publications natural and bestow on them an authority that perhaps they do not deserve. A thorough understanding of the specifics of the design process is vital in being able to analyze all texts more critically.

Hotline's design change, like all changes to objects we are culturally accustomed to, has both positive and negative aspects. In many ways (including its unclear page hierarchy and use of very

www.johnbrownpublishing.com

long lines) the magazine belies its aim to 'appeal to a mass audience'. There is indeed a seemingly irreconcilable tension between the different sections of the magazine, which is only emphasized by the new styles. This conclusion in itself is, however, not such a revelation: there are always ways in which a magazines design can be improved. Design's inherent inability to perform its apparent task and fully convey the meaning of the text means that it is constantly being brought to the fore, to the annoyance of most of the design world's commentators. What is interesting, and what I have shown in my analysis, is how the way that design is appraised provides us with insight into how we read texts.

The emphasis on small lexias of easily accessible information in overlapping windows better supports less continuous blocks of text and the use of the *sans serif* typeface.

This is an obvious acknowledgement to the influence of digital media. New technologies do not support sustained writing. The reader actively engages in the production of meaning by accessing text that leads to not one outcome, but an array of outcomes. Meaning is diffused and text refers not only to concept, but to its own physical presence and relation to many other elements.

The current model used to understand texts draws a distinction between text and design somewhat arbitrarily, and then dismisses design as detrimental to understanding. Design is constructed as an inevitable barrier to meaning that necessarily fails in conveying meanings properly. The barrier metaphor preserves inaccessibility and an illusion that, underneath, the text truly does have a fixed meaning that the reader can potentially master. As a barrier, design provides an excuse to remain distanced from the text, allowing the reader to continue denying the confusing and contradictory nature of textuality.

The conventional model for reading does not, though, exist unchallenged. Digital technologies and the convergence of media are making reading more and more problematic. Hypertext blurs the edges of the conventional text, denying writing its perceived discrete certainty and acknowledging the fact that no two reading experiences can produce the same meaning. As artefacts of this new culture, magazines cannot help but position themselves in relation to it, whether they embrace or deny change. For good or for bad, magazines reflect and influence innovation.

Hi-Fi News

by Paul Prudden

The subject of this project is a comparison between an issue of *Hi-Fi News* and *Record Review* (to be referred to as *HFN/RR*, as it is within the magazine itself) dated June 1990 and the most recent issue (January 2002) of the same title, now more simply titled *Hi-Fi News* (*HFN*). An analysis of the basic style elements in the first magazine will be offered, showing the various components of the design and discussing the layout in relation to the then-existing technology. This will be followed by an account of the changes which are to be seen in the newer issue and the use of the technology now available.

Analysis of the July 1990 Issue of Hi-Fi News and Record Review

The style of the magazine as published in the early 1990s was a contemporary development of the 'special interest' or hobby magazine in print since the 1950s, which tended still to reflect its roots in a relatively amateur (if enthusiastic) culture of cut-and-paste publishing. Although desk-top publishing had been developing for some time by the date of the July 1990 *HFN/RR* issue, the use of this technology had not yet developed sufficiently to allow the production to have escaped that 'amateur' look. The subject matter, high-fidelity stereo equipment, was of particular interest to males of a certain 'boffin' like nature, and indeed this magazine catered to the more technically-minded section of the potential audience. Each article, therefore, had to cover a considerable amount of rather repetitive technical matter, which, in addition to the rather box-like designs of the objects described and pictured throughout, led to a rather linear, thin style which persisted for many years.

There were several other titles covering the subject, most of which took a more consumer-led stance on the matter. This market has shrunk over the years and there are now only a few magazines to choose from.

There were only four different grids used in the July 1990 *HFN/RR*, with the title page being very similar to the predominant three-column layout and the two-column layout being used in only two instances. The vast majority of the editorial and feature content was laid out on a three-column grid (forty-seven found) and some of the record reviews, show reports and small feature/news layouts were made up on four-column grids (nineteen found). All these grids show equal gutter widths and are, therefore, symmetrical designs. There was very little, if any, manipulation of these grids to provide further diversity or variation in the scale of the columns. Complex layouts overlapping the various grids to create diversity were either beyond the means of the publisher at that time or not considered appropriate for the publication. Some pages contain tables that occupy the whole page and these have been compiled individually to accommodate the format, but these pages (fifty-two and fifty-three) could hardly be said to have grid layouts.

Source: *Hi-Fi News* September 2002

The page layout has equal margin sizes (15 mm approximately, though the accuracy of the positioning of the layout on the page is quite variable) to the foot, foredge and back, and a larger margin (20 mm) at the head, which accommodates the various running head styles (see below). This does not accord with the convention of providing a larger foot margin. It illustrates the slightly unfortunate effect this type of layout can induce, leading the eye down to the bottom of the page, as discussed by Paul Honeywill:

> Any element placed on the page at the mathematical centre, optically appears to be below the centre, being pulled downwards (see page 23).

Our visual perception is little understood and the matter of much investigation, but certain values have been identified.

It is generally known that the human eye does not perceive external data in an objective manner, but that certain effects are discoverable. The attraction of the eye to a point below centre on a page is understood, and has brought about consideration of the placement of large, wide and dark images and blocks of text in the lower part of the page and the use, generally, of larger bottom margins, as compensation for this trait (see comments on the gestalt theory of perception below). The back margins are set at an

See R.L. Gregory, *Eye and Brain: the Psychology of Seeing*, 3rd edition (London: Weidenfeld & Nicholson, 1979).

equal width to the foredge, with the result that on the (few) double spreads the central area seems to divide the columns too far, even after allowing for the area of paper lost within the binding. This detail should be considered when margin sizes are selected.

The page furniture includes running heads, predominantly set in reversed black and white in filled boxes bleeding off the page. These are set in approximately 14 pt in a *serif* font, possibly Century Old Style Bold. This is occasionally altered for impact, as seen on page forty-three, which is the lead on page thirty-five, the 'constructional' project. Admittedly, the magazine has always prided itself upon providing expert guidance on home construction of equipment, but this is a signal emphasizing this page over others for no clear reason. Similarly, the show report header is in colour on its first appearance, but most of the other headers in this style are not so emphasized. Adding further confusion is the alternative header, an approximately 28 pt *serif* font (possibly Century Old Style Regular) used in the same space but without a background text box filled with registration/colour. This is used to head some of the long-term regular articles, some, but not all of which, are submitted by well-regarded expert contributors. The first of the letters pages is headed 'Views' in the larger style and then replaced with the filled box style of header on the next page. There seems to be little consistency in this approach, confounding the purpose of running heads in assisting navigation about the identifiable sections of the magazine.

There are other elements of page furniture to be seen, including folios and the magazine title and date, all printed in the lower margin in a very discreet size, so as not to attract the eye away from the main text. It is still questionable as to whether the magazine needs to be identified on every page, but in practice this is not particularly distracting.

Images, both photographs and graphics, are used on most pages to enliven the appearance as well as illustrate the text, but in large part this is done within the columns of the grid, passing up the opportunity to alleviate the regularity of the layouts. A few images, especially on the colour pages, are bled off the page and so add further to the visual interest.

Retro: September 1972

This issue was one of the first after a redesign of the magazine, and it is believed that the new design was not completely implemented at this stage, so that some of the older components were still in place. Unfortunately, no examples are available to confirm this.

The subject matter is, as already stated, of a rather rectilinear design on the whole, and this lack of variety does make the pages seem repetitive and formidable to the casual reader scanning through the magazine. The eye is not as clearly led into the content of the page as it might have been. Captions are rarely used, leaving the reader to identify images from such context as provided by the positioning of the image with regard to the main text. This is compounded by a lack of the use of white space and clear separation of elements in the page or article by sub-headings and other page architecture. Most pages are filled with text and images, and pages containing several articles or reviews are not designed in a manner that would clarify the order and size of each piece. Sub-headings are used too sparingly and the spaces between sections or articles are quite small, requiring the reader to concentrate to find their way about. The main articles are given clear titles (in, for example, 36 pt type) and usually show stand-first explanations of the content (bold, approximately 10 pt), before the author is credited with a rule above and below to help identify the start of the body copy. Dropped capitals (in colour on pages with colour images) lead the eye on, and paragraphs are indented slightly (by about 1 pica em). Long articles are divided into sections that are part of the standard format, but with little regard to the length of the sections, so that large areas of uninterrupted copy are to be found.

The body copy is set in a *serif* font (possibly Garamond Book) set at about 8 pt, and is justified to fit across the columns. This justification has introduced a little of an effect described as 'visual rivers' (sometimes known as 'short measure'), caused by the character spacing leaving too much white space, allowing the eye to be led down through the white spaces on each line instead of along the line of the text. This is not too marked in this magazine, but it occurs occasionally where the balance has not been corrected with hyphenation. There are on average about forty character spaces on each line, and hyphenation has been required as a larger number of technical words and other 'jargon' used in the magazine. This has led to examples of inappropriate and extensive hyphenation, or a tendency to have 'visual rivers' on other pages.

dCS Verdi CD/SACD transpor

Dual-format transport from dCS Limited completes the dig
front-end that connoisseurs have been dreaming about

Magazine design never stands still. In the September 2002 issue the initial dropped capital is replaced by a run-in first line. Athors are now credited with an underscore at the beginning of their name.

WORDS_AUTHOR NAME

auditions

A more sophisticated setup sees the
DAC designated as the master clock

The body copy and display faces are both *serif* font styles and so offer a harmonious effect together, but there is little contrast, which might have been introduced by using a *sans serif* font for headings. Other navigational and design features such as pulled quotes and graphic layout techniques such as runaround (wraparound) text are not used in this issue. Bold type is used, especially in the four-column record review pages, and this is intended to emphasize composers' and musicians' names or otherwise act as sub-headings in a crowded page. This adds to the confusion in most instances as the weight of the characters demands attention when looking over the whole page, but in a rather random and erratic manner.

The content of the July 1990 issue of *HFN/RR* is presented in a manner which was rather conservative but perhaps appropriate for the character of the magazine at that time, but it should be recalled that the technology in use would have allowed much less flexibility than is available today. The overall effect is adequate for the purpose of the magazine, and is recalled to have seemed quite pleasant and interesting, if not particularly original, at the time of publication.

Changes to the House Style as Seen in the January 2002 Issue of Hi-Fi News

In the belief that it is wise to consider the publisher's purpose in producing the magazine, it is important to examine the content of the magazine to discover any changes in emphasis which might account for the design changes that have been made since 1990. The January 2002 issue is a special issue covering industry awards, but this has had little effect on the general layout. The content offers perhaps a little more consumer information, including tables comparing products in price ranges and a dealer guide. This probably reflects a drive to address the competition in this field, which is on the whole more focussed on shopping for equipment than a more objective discussion of high-fidelity sound as a hobby interest.

It should always be remembered that the first objective of a publication is communication, and an awareness of the interests and demography of the potential audience is important to achieve this effectively. It can, therefore, be contended that the new style of the magazine reflects a younger, trend-conscious and consumeristic audience which has been targeted by the publisher. The current format was introduced in October 2000 as a major overhaul of the design in all areas after a lengthy period of gradual minor changes. This analysis will show that the new style is of a more fashionable nature. The magazine has a glossier feel, is printed on a whiter, smoother clay-filled paper and is printed in colour throughout. It has one hundred and thirty-two pages as opposed to one hundred and eight in the older issue.

There is a sophisticated use of grid structures in this issue, with seven different layouts used in combination, reversed and in contrast on spreads. The title page is a special layout which does not conform to the dimensions of any of the layouts within, presumably because of the situation of the masthead on this page and the need to convey a good deal of information and yet retain a welcoming (the title reads 'welcome') front end. There are three two-column layouts, of different alignments and gutter widths, accounting for thirty-six pages. A three-column, evenly-spaced layout is found on twenty pages, an asymmetric two-plus-one layout is found on nine pages and a four-column style on six pages (far less than in the earlier issue). The grids are often interrupted with images, inset text boxes and graphics to add further interest, although just occasionally this does seem to have been taken a little too far.

The margins on the symmetrical pages are set out with 22 mm at the bottom, 18 mm at the foredge and 12 mm at the back margin. These settings address the problems caused by the values used in the older issue, raising the perceived centre of the page to prevent the content 'slipping' down the page and balancing the central white space with the foredge. The head is 25 mm deep, but is generally filled with a medium tone of yellow-brown colour, which also acts to raise the 'centre of gravity' upward on the page. As this is also used as a background for consistent running-head information it has added a decidedly more modern feel. Throughout the magazine, the whole of the header margin area is underlined by a thin rule in black to separate it further from the page. This design has succeeded in separating the navigational information from the body.

Other page furniture includes the folio, printed in bold mid-tone colour but not too conspicuous at about 9 pt, with the month and year printed in light *sans serif* type nearby (so dragging the eye less than before). All of this is included under a graphic and line/rule effect which echoes the oscilloscope screen display icon the magazine has used for some time as a logo (though it no longer appears in the title on the front page). This information is thus linked as one object and placed so as to not disturb the eye while reading the body copy.

There is a greater use of white space throughout the issue and the reversal of grids and so forth emphasize this development. The page has been designed with more care and more options at the designer's disposal. Images, text boxes, graphs and other graphical content are used extensively and in a manner that breaks up the already less constrained design. An interesting tendency is the placement of images of generally rather dull-looking equipment at unusual angles and, wherever possible, using images that break away from straightforward front-elevation photography, allowing some drama with perspective to enhance the page architecture rather than merely illustrate the text.

The headings in the magazine are quite bold and stand out clearly in a good amount of white space. The *sans serif* display font is Helvetica Round set at about 48 pt, which offers a clean line for easy display recognition. *Serifs* have been developed to

Hi-fi radio

assist the eye with deliberate, stylized irregularity to maintain forward progress and allow word recognition without attention to individual characters, which have such familiar shapes to the literate eye. They are not needed for larger sizes and for short line lengths such as are found in headers, and can clutter the appearance at this scale.

The headers show evidence of slight manipulation of the kerning. The characters appear to have been brought a little closer together to improve on the alignment of characters that might not have looked quite right together without adjustment. This brings to mind the words of Adrian Frutiger, who said that 'a small amount of manipulation can give interesting results'.

Stand-firsts are used in many of the main articles, with an additional step between the header and text being found after the

Quoted in Elwyn and Michael Blacker, 'Spoiled for Choice', in Rosemary Sasoon (ed), *Computers and Typography* (Oxford: Intellect, 1993), p. 72.

stand-firsts in the form of a text box containing supplementary information. The body text then commences with an enlarged colour font of similar proportions to the drop capital in the earlier issue, but above the base line, including the first words in the *sans serif* Helvetica Round font face. The type then changes in the longer, denser articles to a *serif* font (believed to be a member of the Dutch family of fonts) of about nine points in size. In shorter and less heavily formatted page layouts the font remains *sans serif*; presumably another version of Helvetica Round. It is apparent that for smaller areas of body text the *sans serif* is not considered too tiring, and a modern, clean look is gained. As the font has quite a high, slender style and is of a light weight, it does provide a rather faint contrast with the white background of the page and it is not ideal for more than a paragraph or two.

Pulled quotes are also used to break up the page and to draw in the reader browsing through the magazine as a whole. This has advantages, but does bring problems with the short measure it makes in each adjacent line as it interrupts the flow of the column as the copy wraps around the text box. The white space and the character spacing are disrupted. The body text is seen to be justified, and, although this produces crisp edges to the columns, it also causes an amount of variation to the spacing in the copy. Some observers feel that:

> There is little apart from tradition to justify justified text . . .
> Justifiying [sic] the text causes unco-ordinated [sic] word spaces whereas unjustified text is the result of coordinating the sign system.

Paragraphs are indented by an em space. The beginning of each of the (still used) traditional sections are not indented, but instead are marked with coloured upper case sub-headings, aligned to the left margin of the column, of a size about 10 pt. These are found after clear breaks in the text to indicate that the sub-heading belongs to the section of copy closer to the sub-heading and below it. This system clearly improves the layout's appearance and the clear navigation of the article.

auditions

Pulled quotes are also used to break up the page and to draw in the reader browsing through the magazine.

Hartley and Burnhill, 'Experiments with Unjustified Text', *Visible Language*, 5:3 (Summer 1971). Quoted in Rosemary Sassoon. 'Through the eyes of a child: perception and type design', in Sassoon, *Computers and Typography*, p. 153.

The text boxes mentioned above are used to add supplementary information in a more visually interesting manner. The text in the supplemental boxes is not justified, as it would probably form too short a line, especially as there needs to be a little clear space around the characters. The text is small, about 7 pt, and the Helvetica Round font is used again. It is white on the dark background of the box and is reasonably clear, though this style would be unpleasant if used for any larger body of copy.

Paul Honeywill identifies four basic elements of design: 'headings, body text, images and white space'. The new design shows consideration of all of these elements and of their use to help the reader to navigate through the magazine.

Conclusion

The 'classical rules' for design found in textbook accounts of the development of design would seem too expensive and inflexible for modern publishing. Today's work is more complex, though not necessarily better in any way. Each generation does what it can with the available technology and the demands of the business in hand.

It is obvious that the use of multiple and overlapping grids allows more expression and freedom to impose broader navigation paths on a publication. White space is today more commonly used to create a lighter feel, with more emphasis on images and navigational tools than text alone would offer. The July 1990 issue of *HFN/RR* is dominated by the text, with a few images and graphics mostly serving to illustrate the text. The new issue employs white space, text (including blocks of copy, text boxes, headers, pull-quotes, and so on), and images (including graphical images) to create a modern feel in accord with the design of most contemporary magazines.

Quoted in Alan Marshall, 'A typographer by any other name', in Sassoon, *Computers and Typography*, p. 139.

This 'modern feel' may reflect something of 'the decline of the printed word' predicted by Marshall McLuhan, who argued that:

> The 'linear' culture of the printed word would soon have to make way for a richer, more complex culture based on the image.

McLuhan's ideas have been scorned as the sudden demise of printing and the 'linear' culture (the thread of our Western culture since the Renaissance) failed to occur, but it could be argued that a gradual shift from text to images (and text as image) is evident in this comparison. Modern 'readers' are often just 'looking' at a magazine, and images are used in a much more sophisticated way, both in this magazine and generally.

Graphics are used sometimes just for the sake of fashion, sometimes countering the intention to communicate by adding too much clutter to a layout, as with pages seventy-two to seventy-three of the *HFN* January 2002 issue. Here text is manipulated to form graphic elements that offer inadequate contrast to the copy printed in front of the graphic swirls and which distract the eye from the already difficult task of reading white text on a dark background. It is not even clear if the text at the top right of the spread is intended to be part of the information or simply decorative, without studying the (as it turns out) graphic and comparing it with the body copy. This sort of design can, however, offer a smart design solution to enlivening a small amount of copy with a background (perhaps corporate) message.

It is easy to suggest that the new design is much more sophisticated than the old, but *HFN/RR* is remembered as a good-looking magazine in 1990 too, so it must be remembered that all such judgements are relative. Some change is just a matter of fashion and not really identifiable by objective study of the processes used to achieve the particular results. It is not just a technical matter; such analysis does not explain finally why the newer issue looks as it does. To some extent there is progress in our understanding of the purpose of design, but there is also just 'progress' which is very much just a matter of fashion.

It would seem from comparison with other IPC group magazines (*Country Life*, *Yachting World* and *Amateur Photographer* were considered) that there are a few 'guru' designers who are brought in by the publisher to establish a house style, not only for the magazine but across the company's publications as a whole. Internet publishing may be accelerating this 'corporate' feel to a good deal of contemporary design, as the ability to jump from one web page or part of a site to another allows the quick recognition of a pattern, or lack of one. Large complex sites must be coherent and designers have been made more aware than ever of this need. The design-by-template style with corporate, rather than in-house, boundaries for that style is unlikely to be abandoned for the time being.

The main objective of any communication is to allow recognition of various components of the design as information, and to facilitate the 'reading' (a contentious word used in its broadest sense) of signs on a 'page' (is a wall covered with graffiti a page?), rather in the manner described by the 'gestalt' school of psychology describing the recognition of patterns, or shapes from a context or background. Wertheimer, in writing about what he called the 'phi phenomenon' or 'apparent motion' described the movement perceived when viewing still images in succession, like a 'movie'.

Other gestalt theorists examined illusions such as the visual reversal of the famous candlestick/two faces image and observed the manner in which such stimuli create more than the constituent parts can convey when seen alone. The Gestalt school found that the brain is capable of learning to recognize new ways of indicating that a communication is being made as such, rather than just learning specific means or systems of communication. It may be argued that the gradual changes in design that can be shown to take place over a period of time (a decade in this instance), may allow the audience to adapt to quite different stimuli without causing any difficulty in the recognition of the 'figure-ground' relationship, or that people learn new ways to receive information. Thus McLuhan's much-dismissed vision of the 'death of Gutenberg' may, in fact, be a slow death, happening even as we fail to notice it.

There does seem to be considerably more emphasis on gathering information via visual cues other than the printed word and this has been accelerated by the Internet user's self-conscious adoption of icons, the graphic novel, the evolution of TV continuity and general content editing, 'scratch' editing and so forth.

We should not ignore, either, the difference between optical character recognition (OCR) and 'reading'. Cognitive psychologists have used analogies based on computing operations to discuss human psychology, but recognize clearly that OCR is not equivalent to perception. The development of new signs and symbols is not a matter of explaining the vectors of the graphics to a new audience, but rather an educational process involving an explanation of the medium and how to recognize it and its content. 'Reading' a brand image or icon need not imply an activity beyond the recognition capacity of OCR, but reading (in the more limited sense of gathering the information contained in a 'text' through whatever process is thought to be occurring) implies a deliberate, active searching rather than a passive reception of information.

The whole design of a magazine can be seen as a convention, setting out rules for the understanding of the magazine's format, which can then be 'subverted' to allow an almost subliminal degree of visual interest. This 'subversion', of course, should not be so dominant as to destroy the sense of there being a convention to be 'subverted' in the first place, or else the content cannot be understood. Overly complex manipulation of the convention(s) can destroy the sense of position and meaning upon which pattern-recognition depends. The point of the exercise is undermined if the design is allowed to become too complex, or to interfere with the simple recognition of characters and images, as happens when contrast between the elements is lost and the harmony of the layout is too radically disrupted.

Design is a complex matter requiring an awareness of the audience, the medium/media to be employed and the desired nature of the communication to be achieved. Detailed consideration of the effects of design decisions on page layout and formatting are of importance and interest to publishers, designers and communicators.

She and Real Simple

by May Yao

It is the prime objective of every magazine to make a profit or to inform its audience. Most magazines strive to do both. The editorial content is, of course, vital to these objectives. The character of a magazine, necessary to distinguish it from its competitors, is determined by its editorial policy, content and style. It is the designer who gives that character an instantly recognizable face. The designer's role is to bring together the editorial content and the reader.

In his book *Designing for Magazines,* Jan V. White explains that we don't 'say', but 'show' in publishing. 'Designers are the interpreters'; it is the design of a magazine that makes the material (text and images) available to the consumer. An analysis of two successful magazines (*She* and *Real Simple*) and how their designers have managed to create and maintain a recognizable, effective face for the respective magazines, will provide insight into this interpretative role of the design of a magazine.

When considering the design of any magazine, it is vital to be constantly aware of, and to understand its target audience. The aim of successful magazine design is to stimulate the reader and to be applicable to its audience. An analysis of the reader must therefore be an essential first step in any design decision process.

Real Simple is an American publication, targeted towards the North American market. The magazine describes its readers as 'intelligent, accomplished, confident, contemporary women' with an average age of thirty-eight years. 'A balanced, manageable and enjoyable lifestyle' and 'personal satisfaction' are important to her. The magazine covers the following categories: Home, Health, Food, Money, Clothes, Looks and Family.

She is a British publication, targeted towards the UK market. It describes its readers as 'intelligent, confident, caring, self-aware

Jan V. White, *Designing for Magazines: Common Problems, Realistic Solutions* (New York: R. R. Bowker Co., 1982), p. ix.

www.realsimple.com

www.she.co.uk

women with a sense of humour'. With an average age of thirty-four, they are 'stylish and indulgent, but never lose sight of reality'. The magazine covers the following categories: Homes, Health, Food, Travel, Fashion, Beauty and Relationships.

Perhaps the most obvious choices that the designers have made with respect to *She* and *Real Simple* are those that relate to the overall format of the publication.

She has a cover that is printed on high gloss paper. It uses a bright spot colour to distinguish its brand name. With two hundred and thirty-two pages, approximately one hundred pages are advertisements (about 43%). *She* is very similar in its overall presentation to the many other women's magazines in the market. It competes on the shelf to attract the eye and the potential consumer's interest. Bold, bright colour, an image of a glamorous woman making eye contact with the reader, plenty of lead-ins and a product incentive all lure the reader towards it and away from its competition. The cover is also the first indication of the magazine's content. *She's* cover indicates clearly that it is a women's glossy magazine covering relationships, fashion, beauty, home and food.

Source: *She*
December 2001

Real Simple is shorter and wider in size than *She*, with dimensions of 228 mm by 276 mm, compared to 215 mm by 290 mm for *She*. It is printed on matte paper, and does not use spot colours anywhere in the publication. With one hundred and fifty-two pages, approximately fifty-seven pages are advertisements (about 38%). Spot colours are not necessary to distinguish the logo of the magazine, because the colours change every issue, depending on the season and the focus of that issue. The brand name is always in two colours, however, and always in the same typeface and location, to provide familiarity and a recognizable face. The cover image often features objects or environments rather than women. If the cover does feature an image of a person, it is taken at a distance and without the direct eye contact that characterizes most women's magazines. Because of this, *Real Simple* is a magazine that is difficult to categorize. It is sometimes placed with the women's magazines, sometimes with lifestyle or homes magazines. The type of image that exists on *Real Simple's* cover is the first indication that it is a magazine with a different approach to communicating with the reader.

Source: *Real Simple*
December 2001

The target audience and content of *Real Simple* and *She* are, then, very similar, and yet the design approach of these two magazines to attract and communicate with its readers is drastically different. This is because the two magazines have very different characters or flavours associated with their brand. While *Real Simple* uses a neat, pared-down aesthetic, *She* explodes with flashy, glamorous dynamism. This variation in aesthetic sensibilities is probably due to the geographical separation of their target audience, and the preferences of those markets. In any case, the result of this variation in aesthetics is a slight shift in the focus of the magazine, which defines its target market and gives it a competitive edge over others. The character of a magazine is established with the preferences and desires of the target audience in mind. Each aspect of the design of these magazines reflects the character as well as the function of the publication.

Grid Structure

When considering the layout of a magazine, designers have to steer a tricky course between providing an atmosphere of comfortable familiarity and inflicting one of boring uniformity. The layout must be recognizable and functional. Ronald Walker, in *Magazine Design: A Hands-On Guide*, even goes so far as to say that 'once established, this structure should not be changed without good reason: it provides that basis of familiarity which is a major step towards reader loyalty'. Despite this, the layout must also remain flexible in order to allow for variation and adaptability.

Ronald Walker, *Magazine Design: A Hands-On Guide* (London: Blueprint, 1992), p. 3.

The main objective of a well-planned layout is the establishment of maximum readability together with an overall sense of scale. According to Paul Honeywill, 'the grid structure is one of the most important design features in achieving a successful layout. It defines the selective positions for the four basic elements of page design: headings, body text, images and white space' (see page 22).

It is common for magazines to have up to twelve grid structures, used alone (sometimes inverted) or overlapped. This complexity is desirable in order to provide visual disruption and variation to avoid static balance in relation to the page edges. Grid variation and flexibility is also useful when fitting advertising and editorial content into the format of the magazine. A higher number of columns within a grid leads to greater flexibility for the designer, as more variations of picture width are possible. This flexibility can often come at a typographic cost. With more columns to a page there must be fewer characters per line of type, which, if drastic, can decrease readability. Grid variations are also used to distinguish between various sections of a magazine, thus improving the overall readability of the publication.

She uses grids of two, three and four columns, three and four being the most common. The three- and four-column grid structures are used extensively throughout the magazine, but with one column often deviating three or four millimetres from the grid. The grids are also inverted in some page layouts. These techniques provide variation to the pages of *She*, while maintaining a general, identifiable grid structure. Boxes that do not follow grids are used to distinguish unrelated information (or information of a different hierarchical level). This approach is successful in creating a dynamic look, but can sometimes result in a page appearing too busy. Grids are not used as a primary means of defining sections, as the same grids are used repeatedly for sequential features.

Real Simple employs a much greater variety of grids. Approximately six different grid structures (of one, two, three and four columns) are used, sometimes inverted, sometimes overlapped. Unlike *She*, *Real Simple* uses its grid structure to define sections of the magazine. The Simple Info section, for example, always uses the same four-column grid, with the two inner columns being used for additional information (pulled quotes, captions, asides and so on). *Real Simple* has to a certain degree sacrificed qualities that make its grid identifiable for variation and flexibility, but the pages maintain their recognizable face using other techniques, such as the consistency of fonts and the use of white space.

In both *She* and *Real Simple*, the grid has been designed with the ambitions of the magazine in mind, and how it chooses to communicate these ambitions with its audience. The grid is what provides the environment for the content. Both magazines, using different techniques, succeed in keeping the grid familiar, while remaining dynamic and exciting.

Alignment

Robin Williams, *The Non-Designer's Design Book* (Peachpit Press: California, 1994), p. 27.

The principle of alignment, according to Robin Williams' *The Non-Designer's Design Book*, states that nothing should be placed on the page arbitrarily. Every item should have a visual connection with something else on the page. It is alignment that helps to create a stronger cohesive unit.

Ranged-left text (used in *She*) and justified text (used in *Real Simple*), are the only practical alignment solutions for a column of text. Ranged-left text was probably chosen for *She* because it results in even word spaces, smoother greyness and less hyphenation, which all improve readability. Static balance is avoided and a sense of dynamism is achieved by the irregularity of the ragged edge of the right-hand margin. The use of justified text in *Real Simple* has been selected, at the expense of readability, to create an overall sense of harmony and calm, taking into consideration the essence of the magazine. Both magazines use ranged-right, centred and sliding type for pulled quotes, titles and other shorter text groups.

46

simple info

Real Simple contents page column.

Page Hierarchy

Designers use several techniques in order to establish page hierarchy, and to consciously direct the reader around the page. Page hierarchy aids readability, allowing the reader to quickly decide whether they wish to continue reading the article as they are drawn in layer by layer.

Real Simple uses a clear reading order, which remains consistent throughout the publication. Photos initially attract the eye of the reader, followed by headings, which grab attention because of their contrasting colour, large size and bold type. Sub-headings, also in colour and in a size that indicates its position in the reading order (smaller than headings but larger than main text), are the next elements to capture the reader's attention.

In *She*, the reading order is similar to that of *Real Simple*, but without the same kind of consistency throughout the magazine. The order is, on many pages, less clear. Elements such as images, headings, sub-headings, pulled quotes, all compete aggressively for the reader's attention. This results in more rapid scanning and is used because there is often more than one feature on a page.

Margins

According to Paul Honeywill, for single column books:

> The largest margin should always be at the foot (bottom) of the page, and the smallest margin should normally always be the back margin (between pages) . . . Publications where the foot is not the widest margin tend to give a visual appearance of the text falling off the page.

Magazines, such as *Real Simple,* do not follow book design principles. Magazines have many columns, therefore the arrangement needs to change. The top margin is the largest, followed by the foot and both foredge margins, which are all approximately equal. This has been done perhaps to allow space for running heads at the top of the page, or to create a feeling of space (using the margin as white space at the top of the page). Also, images are often bled to the top edge, which visually compensates for the larger margin. According to *Magazine Design: A Hands-On Guide* by Ronald Walker, 'tight margins will give an overall dark cast to the pages. A lighter look can be built in by using wider margins, or perhaps adding a narrow column which could be used for side-heads, pictures, graphics or captions.' This is exactly what has been done by the *Real Simple* designers. Because the outer columns are often used for additional information, they are in some ways margins in themselves, making the foredge margins appear equal to both back margins.

In *She* the top margin is again the largest, followed by the back margin, the foredge margin and finally the foot. Again, this is often compensated for by images that extend into the top margin. There are very few double-page spreads, and pages are usually faced by an advertisement. The larger back margin serves as a visual separation between the feature and the advertisement.

Typeface

She uses a *sans serif* typeface in headings, sub-headings, body text and running heads. *Sans serif* typefaces are generally thought to be more difficult to read, but give a modern and vertically-oriented effect. Differentiation between these forms of text is

In *She* the top margin is again the largest, followed by the back margin.

Ronald Walker, *Magazine Design: A Hands-On Guide,* p. 23.

SNUGGLE DOWN
Butter-soft denim, cosy socks, sheepskin boots... roaring fires... flannel PJs... feel toasty warm on a chilly day

made by using bold, italic and colour. Because all fonts used are *sans serifs*, they are in concordance with each other.

Real Simple uses more typeface variation. Body text is always done in a slab-serif typeface. *Serif* typefaces are more traditional, and are generally thought to be less tiring to the eye, providing easier reading. They possess a horizontal momentum, which helps tie the letters together, allowing the eye to move smoothly along the line. Headings and sub-headings are often done in a *sans serif* typeface, sometimes in capitals. Because the fonts used are very different, they contrast each other. Colour is used to define groups of type and reading order, as well as adding to the overall page composition. Colour is also used in the body text of *Real Simple*, usually with muted or toned-down hues. In *She*, body text is always black.

When considering the size of type for the body text, it is useful to consider the age of the reader. Paul Honeywill states that 'the reader's eye will tire if the body size for a large amount of text appears smaller than 9 pt or larger than 14 pt.' *She* uses 9 pt type for its body text, which is in compliance with the above statement. *Real Simple*, however, uses 8 pt type for its body text. This design decision was perhaps made in order to create a more solid grey hue to the page.

Headings

Real Simple headings are usually in colour, which differentiates them from other forms of text. A larger font size and different typeface are also often defining factors. *She* uses colour in headings as well, or sometimes a combination of black and colour, with one word in black and one in red, for example. These words in different colours are sometimes overlapped; a technique used as an identifiable characteristic of *She*. Some *She* headings are in upper case, some in lower, and some in combination; consistency is surrendered for the sake of variation. Headings are often placed in the right top corner of the page, touching the page edges. This is another design technique for creating a graphic identity for *She*, but the result is perhaps at the expense of clarity. The heading in this position can easily be confused with the running head or the section heading, and can disrupt the reading order of the page.

Sub-Headings

She sub-headings are usually in upper-case characters, in a larger font size than the body text. They are generally in a heavier font than the body text, but not as heavy as the heading font. All these characteristics successfully define the position, importance and reading order of the sub-heading on the page.

Real Simple sub-headings, similarly, possess characteristics which define their relationship to other forms of text on the page. Although they are usually in the same typeface as the body text, they are larger and often in colour. Again, they are in a heavier font than the body text, but lighter than that of the heading.

Stand-first Line

In *Real Simple*, stand-firsts are usually in a contrasting font to the heading and sub-heading. Sometimes they are defined by colour, such as the light grey that is used for the stand-firsts of the Simple Info section. This light grey is not conducive to readability, but serves the overall compositional character of the page and the magazine. The designers have maintained its position in the reading order through its font size and leading. The characters are spaced out, which improves readability and attracts the eye.

She stand-firsts are usually in a *sans serif* typeface, similar to its headings and sub-headings. They differ from headings because of their lighter and smaller font. Unlike *Real Simple*, *She* stand-firsts are always in black.

Pulled Quotes

Pulled quotes in *She* are sometimes in bold colour (often the same as the heading), which visually breaks up the greyness of the body text. Alternatively, they are within coloured boxes which provide the same result, or in bold black text, distinguishing it from the body text. In any case, they are surrounded by a sufficient amount of white space to indicate that they are a separate form of text.

Real Simple always uses colour to differentiate pulled quotes. Quotes are often not placed within the main body text, but to the side (below illustrations or in the margins). This technique creates a simplified, streamlined effect, which corresponds to the overall feel of the magazine.

I'M DREAMIN

THIN CI

1 For you, does a happy Christmas depend on fitting into your littlest black dress? Here, one woman tells of her own "fat" and "thin" years

FEATURE RONNA LICHTENBERG

2 Organisation point, so we that I always planning for by the end of August, I'm one of those enviab buys presents months b needs them. No, I made on what I expected to Christmas, using every and lose 1½lb a day, I 2 stone I need to lose b of the year.") I'm one of whose weight has alwa and down – since I'm it didn't have to go up very much before it c self-perception enough to change my Christ Christmas is the time when you've got to wear little (or big) black dresses to festive p smile for the camera. You have to chat chee deal with your family and meet up with pea you've not seen all year. If there is any cons barometer of your weight, this is it. Look ba Christmas photos from the last ten years, ai instant snapshot of your life in pounds. It se I realise that what I weigh – and, more impe feel about what I weigh – has made a big d during the Christmas break. It influences wh how enthusiastically I'm able to celebrate w and friends, the presents I give and the one What I weigh has mattered a great deal.

Take wardrobe decisions on New Year's E night when the world agrees that if you've all to flaunt, you should be flaunting it. Wh OK weight (I can't remember ever thinking weight") the plan was always to wear as litt so in thinner years I've sported spaghetti-st

She:

1) Stand-first line.

2) Initial Letter (drop cap).

3) Pulled Quote.

cleavage-enhancing tops with extremely high-heel
shoes. But in the 'fat years', my plan was to cover up as
much as possible. For example, there was the New Year's
Eve I wore a strange vintage kimono I'd been given
years before and never had the energy to throw away.
As unbecoming as it was, it was better than the
prospect of going shopping and seeing my bountiful
bottom in a three-way mirror. Worse still was the
New Year's Eve I was in such a blob that I convinced friends
we should celebrate with
a quiet night in. The evening
turned out to be so quiet
that by the time the clock
struck midnight we were all
in flannel nighties.

By the millennial New Years
Eve, I was in such a flap
about my weight that
I convinced the same friends
we'd have fun bringing in the
next century at a fat farm,
drinking low-calorie sparkling
wine and limiting our main
courses to crudites.

Then there are all the other
celebrations of the season. In
years when I was at my peak
weight, or had just set a new
peak, I figured that I might as
well eat what I wanted – after

"In thinner
years, I wore
spaghetti
strap tops –
as little as
possible"

all, it just meant adding a few numbers to the perennial
New Year's Eve resolution to lose Xlb. So not only did
I happily accept gifts of Christmas sugar cookies but
I also ate them for breakfast. I drank eggnog and went
to pizza parties, tried the cheesecake chocolate
brownies that someone's aunt had sent and generally
said an enthusiastic "yes" to everything. I just fled it by
thinking how happy it made everyone else that I was ▶

Running Heads and Folios

She does not use running heads to help the reader to orient themself within the magazine. It can be quite confusing and difficult to determine which section of the magazine you are looking at. Perhaps it was assumed by the designers that most readers flip through the magazine, stopping to read features that catch the eye, and running heads are therefore not necessary. Even if this is the case though, the lack of running heads makes it difficult to locate a particular section. The folio consists of the magazine website www.she.co.uk placed to the right of the page number in the bottom left corner. This is an effective technique to advertise the magazine's online presence, while still serving the purpose of the folio by indicating the title of the publication. The folio is not, however, located on every page. Many pages that contain full-page images do not have the page number and folio, presumably so that the image has a stronger, more effective visual impact. The inconsistency of folios can be frustrating, however, when searching for a specific page.

Real Simple uses quite an extensive running head for its Simple Info section, but does not use running heads in the rest of the magazine. The Simple Info section, a constant feature in the magazine, is thus easy to identify for regular readers. Other sections are differentiated by their grid structure, as previously mentioned. Folios are located on most pages (they are missing from occasional full-image pages and advertisements). It is perhaps because *Real Simple* has fewer full-page images that it is much more consistent with folio placement.

Initial Letters

Initial letters in *She* are much larger than the body-text size, usually spanning three to five lines in height and of a very heavy font. Sometimes the initial letter is also in a bold colour. These characteristics emphasize the starting point of the feature, drawing the reader into the body text. The colour makes the initial letter an obvious part of the overall page composition.

Real Simple does not use initial letters. This decision was perhaps made in an effort to simplify the overall appearance of the page, but the result is that the reader is not drawn into the main text. For the layout to carry out its function successfully, it relies on the reader to make the effort and assumption of starting to read the main text at the top left corner. In the Simple Info section an alternative approach is made. A vertical coloured line along the left side of the body text serves a similar purpose to the initial letter by drawing the eye up to the top left corner of the text. A simple, streamlined effect is also achieved with this vertical line.

White Space

White space can add elegance to a spread. According to Ronald Walker, it allows the design to breathe, and can direct attention to an important aspect of the message. The overall sense of simplicity and calm that makes *Real Simple* so distinctive would not have been possible without the tactful use of white space. White space is used on nearly every page to create a feeling of spaciousness and rest. White space is also used in *She*, but because a very different effect is desired, it is used more sparingly and in a different way. *She* uses white space to distinguish various forms of text, or on pages where multiple features exist, to indicate that the various features are not related to each other.

Ronald Walker, *Magazine Design: A Hands-On Guide*, p. 48.

Images

She's use of images is quite conventional for a women's magazine, with lots of full-page, eye-catching images, many of women looking at the camera (a popular advertising technique). In addition, there are many images of objects (in the Food section, for example), and places (in the Homes section). On pages that contain a collection of many small features, several images often appear. This creates a busy, almost collaged effect that is exciting and dynamic, but confuses the reading order.

Real Simple images rarely feature women looking directly at the camera. If they do, they are generally doing something simultaneously (gardening, for example). Although models are used, recognizable, well-known faces rarely appear on the pages of *Real Simple*. This is in keeping with the objective of the magazine to keep things realistic and attractively pared down. The images exude a feeling of calm and quiet confidence.

In *She* eye contact is maintained, whereas *Real Simple* rarely feature women looking directly into the camera.

Captions

Captions in *She* are typically in black, and exist as a column to the left, right or below the image. They are in the same font as the body text, often in bold type, and are placed within a coloured box, or layered on top of the image. Similarly, *Real Simple* captions appear to the right, left or below the image and in the same font as the body text. In *Real Simple* they are differentiated by square brackets.

Conclusion

The audience is of prime importance in the creation of a magazine. The editorial content must be written with the desires and requirements of the readers in mind, but must also correspond with the expectations of those readers for the particular title. Because the magazine market is so saturated, there are countless magazines targeting similar audiences and promising similar content, often with a slightly different focus. The magazines examined here are good examples of this. They must compete on the basis of how their content is presented, which is essentially dependent on their design. *She* and *Real Simple* approach this communication issue in very different ways. According to Walker:

Ronald Walker, *Magazine Design: A Hands-On Guide*, p. 71.

> Unfortunately, there are publishers who are nervous about allowing designers the freedom to express that essential cover-to-content connection in any but conventional and hackneyed ways. How many hundreds of anonymous, female faces have stared out at us from the racks devoted to women's interest magazines?

This is possibly true in the case of *She*, which approaches its design in a relatively conventional way. It is not so much the content, as the design that defines the brand and the character of the magazine. *Real Simple*, with similar content to *She*, delivers its information in a unique way because of its design. Whether conventional or unique, any design decision affecting the various page components examined earlier will directly influence the effectiveness of the magazine in achieving its primary objectives of making a profit and informing its audience.

CLASSIC FM

Source: *Classic FM*
February 2001

Source: *Empire*
November 2000

THE TOP
née
ing

"Come and share my music"

Callas lives!
Henry Kelly meets TV's

Win

**EVERY NEW FILM
Reviewed**

◁SEXIEST
EVER PICTU

NOVEMBER 2000
£2.90

EMPIRE

empireonli

**And even
more sex!**

69

Oh,
horr

Empire and Classic FM

by Alison Evans

Allen Hurlbert, *Publication Design: A guide to page layout, typography, format and style* (Wokingham, Berkshire, Van Nostrand Reinhold, 1976), p. 40.

Design is the essential creative process in a publication, 'a creative and intuitive action that brings editorial ideas into focus with reader involvement.' The designer's challenge is to engage the reader and continue to hold their interest. The difficulty lies in creating visual surprises so that the magazine is constantly evolving, while retaining a degree of ease, order and familiarity for the reader's comfort. As well as enticing new readers, the designer has to hold onto current ones and persuade them to continue as regular readers, despite offers from magazines elsewhere in the field. The final result should appear effortless and attractive.

By analyzing the design of *Empire* and *Classic FM*, two well-established and respected publications in the field of entertainment, it is possible to assess whether the content met the needs of its readers right across the market, and whether the visual layout, regarding text, image and typographic design, were put to effective use.

The issues examined were dated November 2000, although reference will also be made to *Empire's* October 2000 issue and *Classic FM's* February 2001 issue in order to properly discriminate between the separate principles both magazines employ to achieve a visual and textual connection with the reader. The essential aim of any publication is to communicate and the objective was to examine whether the design of either magazine helped readers engage with and perceive the message being conveyed. In December 2001, *Classic FM* underwent a major re-design. The art director kindly answered my questions in hindsight and explained the reasons behind the changes.

The factors that influence a reader are relevance, design, quality, format, content and advertising. The basis of magazine publishing is the search and selection of information for its audience.

According to Allen Hurlbert, 'no matter how large or small a magazine's audience is, no mater how it is distributed, or how often each copy changes hands, that audience is made up of individuals, and the significant exchange takes place only when each individual picks up his copy and opens its pages.'

Allen Hurlbert, *Publication Design*, p. 40.

The reputation of any magazine is derived from its coverage of the subject, its style and its accuracy. A magazine should have its own unique design, which is itself a product of a market that needs to be identified. Both perfect-bound, *Empire* and *Classic FM* command predominantly male audiences, but the ages of their audiences vary greatly. Whilst *Empire* readers are aged between sixteen and thirty, over 50% of *Classic FM* readers are aged over fifty-four, although the art director stressed that they aim for readers aged over forty.

The art editor of *Empire* explained that the magazine had been launched in April 1989 with the aim to deliver 'glamorous and exclusive pictures every month' and to be 'packed with star interviews and features on the latest film releases'. *Empire* 'celebrates film and has unrivalled access to the film industry, giving you compulsive, behind-the-scenes coverage of the stars and their movies.' Staff are particularly proud of the recent addition, Public Access, a popular section in which readers send in the questions themselves.

Telephone interview with art director of *Empire* (25 November 2000).

According to the media pack, *Empire's* brand values are glamorous, celebratory and in-the-know. Glamour is instantly recognizable in the *Empire* logo, a typeface specially designed for the magazine. A rounded version of its straight predecessor from 1989, the logo is red, bold and chunky, spot-varnished with a very subtle drop-shadow. The colour red complements the sexy theme to *Empire*, whilst the bold, eye-catching effect of the logo represents cool seriousness.

Since its launch in April 1995, *Classic FM* has maintained well-balanced content from legendary composers to famous musicians and new stars. The art director explained that 'by putting features together like this in the same magazine, the message to the reader is hopefully that we are covering all angles of the subject in depth.' In terms of design, *Classic FM* demonstrates 'that there is a sensitivity to the subject and that there is also a change of page

Email from art director of
Classic FM
(17 January 2001).

throughout the magazine, [with] less likelihood of the whole becoming bland, providing many entry points so that it can be dipped in and out of.' Like *Empire's* Public Access, staff are particularly proud of a new feature to the re-design, 'What's the fuss about...', in which a musician, who has entered recent controversy, is interviewed.

Classic FM use a sophisticated font for their logo; Bauer Bodoni is a *sans serif* typeface. The logo is white with a subtle drop-shadow, interrupted by a bolder, italicised f in small case. The f is coloured red, like *Empire's* logo, simultaneously aligning with its sexy cover star, Vanessa Mae, whilst creating visual elegance with a roman versus italic typeface.

John Wharton, *Managing
Magazine Publishing*
(London: Blueprint, 1992).

John Wharton notes that 'there have to be recognition symbols for regular, committed readers – title, format, cover style – while for new readers there has to be something which captures their initial interest – usually the cover picture – and then entices them to buy.' A magazine cover must sell itself whether on the shelves of a newsagent, a coffee table, an office desk or a waiting room. Major stars in their fields appear on the covers: actor Harrison Ford and violinist Vanessa-Mae. Ford is centred, a close-up of his face and shoulders against a desert background, with teasers either side. The teaser to the left of his face advertises the feature of 'the 69 horniest characters of all time.'

Surprisingly, for a mainly elderly audience, *Classic FM* risks a semi-nude Mae against a deep purple background, wearing a light blue low-cut gown and black cowboy hat, covering her bare chest with her arms. Both magazines cleverly interweave part of the cover star's image into their design. Ford is dressed in black with an aggressive frown on his face, against a background familiar from his *Indiana Jones* films. According to the *Classic FM* art designer, 'the Vanessa-Mae feature was devised to reflect her personality; the photographer will have been specifically selected for his ability to capture Vanessa in this way and the end result of the shoot will have directed the layout of the pages. A feature like this is reliant on the commissioning of the correct photographer and good art direction. It is always preferable to do this. With current artists who are nowadays marketed much more like pop stars and handled very closely by the record label they are signed to. Shooting them ourselves allows us to get the right image and portray them as we would like to our readers: in this case young and sexy.'

Email from art director of *Classic FM* (17 January 2001).

Classic FM tries to attract a younger audience with Mae as their cover star, whilst teasers introduce names older readers will be familiar with: violinist Yehudi Menuhin and Beatles record producer, George Martin. There is a miniature in the bottom left-hand corner to illustrate the enclosed CD of violin prodigies, Mae and Menuhin among them.

The formula for successful page design is the organization of four basic elements; headings, body text, images and white space, and the contrast or harmony of shapes and colours. Other elements, such as the grid and initial letters can all:

> . . . reinforce the reader's feeling of familiarity and, at the same time, help build up that essential, distinctive personality which any successful magazine must possess. The character of a magazine stems from its editorial policy, content and style, but it is the designer who gives that character an instantly recognizable face.

Ronald Walker, *Magazine Design: A Hands-On Guide*, (London Blueprint, 1992), pp. 3-4.

Format

Three-column and four-column grids are predominantly used in both magazines. Often multiple grids are used within the same page, allowing for flexibility. The final look of the page depends on the careful division of white space, with a little imagination brought to the proportions. Hence, no spread is entirely the same in either magazine, producing fresh, engaging pages for the reader, made by only the subtlest change. A sophisticated look comes through subtlety. In *Empire*, the page layouts of the reviews for *Road Trip* and *Dinosaur* are the same in terms of grid structure, image size and rules, only subtle elements are different, such as the pulled quote in *Dinosaur*, which is shorter and snappier, allowing for more white space.

Multiple grid variations in *Classic FM* bring a dynamic appearance to such articles, as in the feature on Schubert, in which the designer is able to include a timeline, captions, separate articles on the top ten recordings and websites, not to mention

Classic FM (November 2000), pp. 28-32.

Classic FM (February 2001), pp. 44-49.

photographs, caricatures and paintings. Ostensibly, the re-design is far simpler, retaining only the top ten recordings with a key list of dates in the composer's life, rather than a timeline. There is one photograph and one painting, whilst a photograph of a bust takes the place of the caricature. This allows the composer to appear formidable and imitates the permanence of his legend. In *Classic FM*, the reader is directed through headings, stand-firsts and images towards the article, with a smaller image preferred to a pulled quote. In *Empire*, the reader is more often directed by large images, then by headings and stand-firsts. Pulled quotes are often added inside or along the image to create an effectively personal feel to the article, as the reader can directly associate the quote with its speaker. *Classic FM* also employ this method but with images further into an article.

Classic FM has an interesting use of captions. For their 'violin prodigies special', captions on violinists from Menuhin to Anne-Sophie Mutter run from pages thirty-eight to fifty, rotated and overlaid with a pastel blue background. Many more articles take this format, the captions varying in size but always in the same blue colour, to establish recognition for the reader and continuity to unify the magazine. Often the captions in both magazines are placed underneath pictures, which the reader will locate by looking at the image first. Alternatively, direction is offered on busy pages such as either magazine's news and gossip features, *Empire's* Front Row and *Classic FM's* The Score. The reader is told to which image the caption refers; left, below, opposite, and so on.

Typefaces

Harry Carter, in *Typographers on Type: An Illustrated Anthology from William Morris to the Present Day*, edited by Ruari McLean (London: Lund Humphries, 1995).

Inside *Empire*, the typefaces visually shout. Inside *Classic FM*, they visually whisper. Whilst *Empire* opts for bold, serious typefaces, *Classic FM* prefers elegant and old-fashioned ones. Two families dominate each magazine. *Empire* use Helvetica and Bembo; clear, distinctive *sans serif* typefaces, of which typographer Harry Carter approves for their durability and for 'providing a compromise between legibility and economy of space, which means quick reading.' Helvetica is used for headings, stand-firsts, body text, and running heads, whilst Bembo is used for the body text of interviews. With the repetitious use of such recognizable and easily accessible typefaces, unity is established and a trendy look achieved for their younger audience. Some features use the typeface specially designed for the film, like the feature on *Blair Witch 2*.

Classic FM makes a contrast between its two families; Bauer Bodoni, a graceful modern font, and Gil Sans, a straightforward *sans serif* font. The contents page effectively demonstrates the different roles these families play, The Regulars section is typed in Gil Sans to indicate formality and order, whilst Features, as in *Empire*, uses Bembo to capture the themes of elegance and nostalgia. Bembo proves difficult to read in *Classic FM* as there is insufficient leading between the lines. Like *Empire's* use of Helvetica, Bauer Bodoni is used consistently throughout the magazine for headings. The art director told me that 'as *Classic FM* is only around the one hundred page mark, hence not many pages for a perfect bound consumer magazine, it is important not to clutter pages up with too many different typefaces and to have a consistency throughout the magazine. For this reason, using the same font is a good idea, so as to keep a strong magazine style and to bring unity to the whole product.'

Unlike *Empire*, which mainly uses black lettering against a white background or vice versa, *Classic FM* relies on the possibilities of colour (besides size, weight, structure, form and direction) to avoid boredom. Typographer Bernard Newdigate called Bauer Bodoni a typeface of 'sweltering hideousness' but added that it does produce a good-looking tone on the page. The use of large size and small-case lettering produces a simpler, distinctive look and makes room for other elements to fit in. With a deep drop capital, the headings are separate and do not obstruct the page. Robin Williams argues that by consistently using the same typeface, 'not only is your page more visually interesting... but you also increase the visual organization and the consistency by making it more obvious.'

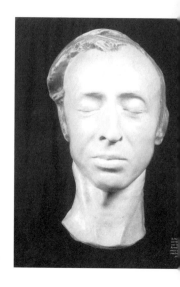

Email from art director of *Classic FM* (17 January 2001).

Bernard Newdigate, in *Typographers on Type*, p. 35.

Robin Williams, *The Non-Designer's Design Book*, p. 45.

Running Heads and Folios

In *Empire*, the running heads and folio use Helvetica. For special features, the *Empire* logo is used. The '69' feature uses a miniature of the double-page spread introduction of Marilyn Monroe's

Classic FM double-page
spread (February 2001).

Email (17 January 2001).

mouth, next to a black box with 'the sexy 69' in white lettering. The folio in the corner includes the magazine name and date. The furniture is smaller than the body text but the folio is emphasized in bold to separate itself from the date. The space between the grid and the foot furniture is greater than one line of body leading, so there is no confusion as to where the body copy ends.

In *Classic FM*, the running head uses Bauer Bodoni, whilst the folios use Gil Sans in a light type which makes it difficult to see. In the Regulars section, there is one running head always in the same pastel blue used for the captions. With Features, there is an additional running head in black for the musician's name, separated by one line of spacing. The vital thing for good typography is clarity. Whilst *Empire* uses the clearest available typefaces, *Classic FM* uses spacing for legibility; in the bottom running head, four spaces are used between letters. For the interview with George Martin, an image of interviewer Henry Kelly and Martin feature alongside the running head.

There is no foot furniture with the folio placed on the side of the page, a quarter of the way down, where the reader's eye will naturally fall. Often advertisements are featured on this side for several pages and when they finish, the folio has suddenly moved to the top corner, leaving the reader confused as to know where to look. According to the *Classic FM* art director, 'the constant ornaments on the page can sometimes be ignored and just used in the conventional and acceptable way, especially running heads and folios. The placing in the November issue on the folio was less conventional and did give a very apparent and easily accessible reference to the reader of where they were in the magazine.' In the re-design, the folios have been moved to the bottom corner of the page and emphasized in bold, as in *Empire*.

Margins

In both magazines, the margins are deep at top and shallow at bottom. *Empire's* side margins are equal when photographs are not bleeding off the page. In *Classic FM*, the body text begins further in, depending on the size of the captions or images. This allows for wider columns and the subtly deceiving appearance for the reader that there is less body text, so reading will not take so long.

Colour

Empire uses bold, striking colours to reflect the brilliant personality of the magazine. Bright reds, yellows and blues feature predominantly throughout as headings and background to smaller articles. Top margins are in a lighter blue with pale grey for stand-firsts and review film titles. A balance between pastel and rich colours is achieved throughout *Classic FM* to continue the theme of quiet sophistication. Pastel blue is used for bottom running heads and captions, whilst headings vary in gold, burgundy, black, brown, orange and pink. Like in *Empire*, a lighter blue is used for top margins and the odd splash of red here and there connotes the logo. Gone are the pastel colours in favour of the darker shades of the re-design, which give a sexy, glossier look.

Ranged Left Type and Justification

Empire uses ranged-left type, which is easier to read and allows white space to make the article breathe. As there are separate typefaces for Regulars and Features, there appear be different alignments for the text in *Classic FM*, ranged-left for Regulars and justified for Features. Although justification appears to be solely used for interviews and articles on major artists, the feature on Schubert is not, whilst a Regular on spotting child prodigies is. According to Robin Williams, the most sophisticated designs are often not centred or justified. Therefore, *Classic FM* does not necessarily have to use justification in order to convey its message.

The art designer of *Classic FM* had her own ideas on justification. 'Justification is all right as long as you have a typeface that is economical, and a fairly wide column width so that you avoid getting rivers running through the text. In this scenario, it can look very neat but it does nothing for the kerning of a typeface, which, in all cases, should be respected. I would not use justification, unless it was for a sidebar that was looking very untidy but even in this case, it should then become a constant style and always used. I prefer ranged-left type as it is more natural and if you have a decent editorial and subbing team, they will sub the copy, so that it doesn't look too ragged on the right anyway.'

Empire double-page spread.

Email from art director of
Classic FM
(17 January 2001).

Clear Hierarchy

Whilst browsing through a magazine, the reader is looking for reasons to stop and read. Headings and images are essential for grabbing the reader's attention. Further interest is sought in stand-firsts and captions. It is very important that the designer ensures that each of these elements work as they should. There must be a very clear hierarchy in each page, so that the reader's eye is directed to the elements in the order that the designer intends.

In *Empire*, a clear reading order is established, with short and succinct headings, which are normally recreations of a film quote or title: for example, 'Beam Me Up Shorty' for a caption on sci-fi shorts. All images have a little joke, mocking what the people in the images are saying. The opening review for the suspense thriller, *What Lies Beneath* features a large photograph, which bleeds off onto the opposite page. A fearful Michelle Pfeiffer wanders around a dark house, trying to prevent her candle from blowing out. The inserted joke reads, 'Why don't I just turn on the lights instead?' Such inventiveness and humour add spark to the magazine as a whole. The pulled quotes are set in a larger and heavier type to set them apart from the body text. They are either sexy or darkly funny, so as to capture the reader's attention and keep within the magazine's tone. Pulled quotes and images make up for one another when either of them is lacking, placed in the middle of paragraphs so that there is a full line of text above and below to determine space.

Classic FM appealing to younger audiences.

A clear hierarchy is evident in *Classic FM* with their headings imitating the flamboyant and musical style and message of the magazine, from 'the original boy wonder' for Menuhin and an appeal for younger audiences, to 'iron maiden' for Vanessa Mae. Articles tend to rely on smaller images rather than pulled quotes but interviews try to use both. As with headings, some pulled quotes are there for younger readers, others for the older. George Martin, whom younger readers may not be familiar with, is quoted 'classical music is now cool, which heartens me more than anything', whilst Menuhin's father speaks of his son: 'Once in every century God in a burst of joyousness sends down a "new soul" – pure, gifted, endowed with heavenly power'.

Sub-Headings

Empire uses three levels of sub-heading the layout of major reviews. The release date and certificate are placed within a black box with white lettering, like 'the sexy 69' running head. 'In a Nutshell' is a summary of the plot in a lighter type and the review ends on 'Any Good?', the critic's final opinion, in the same type as the certificate, only slightly larger. These sub-headings help to alternate the tone of the review and organize it into different sections, so that the reader can have pause for thought.

Classic FM uses two sub-headings in their reviews: one for the type of music and one for a brief meaning of the music. The former is in Gill Sans, the latter in Bauer Bodoni, but of the smallest size, barely legible to the reader. The layout of the reviews is text-based and unimaginative, with the title of the album or composer in bold beginning each paragraph, and the CD covers across the top of the spread. However, each review is brief and written succinctly. In the re-design, the text has been divided into captions with the CD cover at the top, with six clearer headings, so that no meaning is necessary. Indeed, one reader wrote in: 'Congratulations on the new look to the January issue, especially the enlarged letters, cover CD and CD review sections'.

Initial Letters

Even though a clear hierarchy is established within each magazine, the reader still needs guidance. In *Empire*, reviews, major features and interviews all begin with initial letters, varying in size. For major reviews and smaller interviews, the initial letter does not exceed three lines in depth but uses a marginally larger, thinner type than the heading. For major features and star interviews, the initial letter is huge and bold, which can exceed no less than nine lines in depth, four times the size of the heading. This does not interfere with the layout as a whole but instead adds an unusual contrast to the long columns of body text.

In *Classic FM*, all initial letters do not exceed five lines in depth. The first paragraph is always shorter, so that the remaining body text can fit in well. The same rules that applied to justification apply regarding initial letters. For interviews, there are initial letters to assist the reader in finding the starting point, but there

Elisabet
The versatile '80s survivo

The idea of invisibility instantly becomes s
a bit sexual," states Elisabeth Shue. c
"I've been talking to a lot of women 'V
about what they would do if they were ir
invisible, and you'd be surprised at what h
their answers are. Everybody wants to t
watch people having sex." t
Everybody, especially Hollow Man's b
director, one Paul Verhoeven, who has t
imbued this invisibility thriller — in which
Shue assays a fraught co-scientist to Kevin
Bacon's disappearing boffin — with his
predilection for blood, guts, and the
copious flashing and fiddling of

Girl Trouble

Take a debut director and a lo
do you get? One white-hot mo

WORDS GINA MORRIS **PORTRAIT** ST

or the lead role in her
debut feature, a female
Rocky no less, 32 year-old
writer-director Karyn
Kusama was certain
of two things. One: she
wanted an unknown ("We
tested 'name' actresses,
just to say we'd done it,"
she laughs). And two: that unknown would
under no circumstances be Michelle
Rodriguez. "I thought she was crazy," the
director says flatly. "I basically wrote her
off during the auditions. She gave a really
chaotic reading, then told us, 'Being an e
tells you nothing about acting; I hav
experience.' She was such a fu

Empire used initial letters of
varying sizes and weights.

are none for articles. Instead, the opening paragraph begins directly underneath the heading, or sufficient white space above the first one-and-a-half columns is offered as guidance.

White Space

In *Empire* and *Classic FM*, headings and pulled quotes have the most space, in proportion to other elements on the page. *Empire* neatly places its sub-headings below the heading, with minor sub-headings close to the body text, to allow the reader's eye to centre on the article. *Classic FM* is particularly generous with white space. Bleeding off the page, the layout seems bigger, as if the design has been expanded. It also gives the impression that there is not much to be read, due to the immense drop cap used on the titles.

For an older audience, the white space is relaxing, giving them reason and encouragement to turn the page. The double-page spread of The Score slots minor headings into the images to create more white space and room for the body text. Such use of white space helps the article appear neater and evenly balanced. The art director of *Classic FM* commented that 'most designers love their white space. The old style magazine had a larger trim than we do now and allowed for more air in the features. It is helpful to older readers but it is also to create an elegance, which is so often fitting of classical music and also, I have to admit, to indulge the designer a tad too.'

Email from art director of
Classic FM
(17 January 2001).

Images

Both *Empire* and *Classic FM* use a mixture of photographic and illustrative material. As a magazine for visual entertainment, every article in *Empire*, no matter how small, contains an image, either a still from a film or a publicity shot of an actor, director, or similar. However, there are times when the photograph dominates the page to such an extent as to leave other elements little room to breathe. Such is the case regarding the opening review, *What Lies Beneath*, the photograph of Pfeiffer squashing the heading and ratings table to the side of the page.

For a feature on the large cast of *Road Trip*, the reader's eye is guided by arrows to separate boxes from the main group photograph, which has been centred on the fold where there is a gap between the characters. Therefore, the layout does not interfere with other elements. The circled photographs on the box corners, alternating from left to right, help the reader to ensure that they have the right character. *Empire* relates to current entertainment news by inventing their own *Big Brother*, based on the latest live soap opera, featuring selected actors, drawn in cartoon, which reveals humour and a creative effort to engage their readers' interest.

The photographs used by *Classic FM* are as elegant and flamboyant as their magazine style. Never are two images the same size, providing further stimulation for the reader. In the Andrea Bocelli interview, a photograph has been enlarged along the diagonal to create a dramatic portrait of Bocelli. For the Menuhin feature, an image of a violin is placed alongside the heading, the rounded curves of the violin harmonising with the rounded curves of the typeface, Bauer Bodoni. Each interview, as with the article on Schubert, uses a variety of different images to tell the story of the artist's background. In the Menuhin feature, ordinary black and white photographs are given slight tints of colour for variation, so that the type used over the image, indicating his age at the time, can be seen clearly. An early publicity shot from 1936 has been recovered, neatly projecting the old-fashioned image of the magazine.

As in the *What Lies Beneath* review, a photograph of child prodigy violinist Stefan Jackiw bleeds off onto the opposite page. However, like the *Road Trip* article, Jackiw is centred, playing the violin amidst a lush, mountainous background, an imitation of the famous opening of the film *The Sound of Music*. The inserted joke reads 'The hills are alive', similar to *Empire's* use of in-jokes for review images. The last word of the heading, 'the tale of an ordinary genius' is enlarged and covers both the bleed and what remains of white space, so a well-balanced layout is achieved.

Advertising

Empire and *Classic FM* use either full or half-page advertisements on facing editorial pages. As a point of interest, the selection of advertisements in each magazine were listed to see if they reflected the magazine's personality and contributed to bringing

Classic FM interview with Andrea Bocelli.

the message across. Aside from advertisements on film clubs and the latest DVD and video releases, there is a heavy influence of latest technology from widescreen TVs and DVD players to Seiko watches and computer games. According to the media pack detailing their reader's lifestyles, 'they are interested in latest technology, internet, DVD etc. but aren't obsessed by it.' The choice of computer game underlines the magazine's theme of sex, with Kouldelka's 'the sexiest gothic horror role playing game.' The advertisements are mainly directed towards men, the vast majority of *Empire's* audience, from Ralph Lauren jeans to aftershaves, as are videos such as *Get Carter*, the 1970s detective TV series *Sweeney*, and the films of Robert De Niro.

The choice of advertisements in *Classic FM* reflect the quiet life of the cultured reader. There is an indication of the audience's age with a large advertisement for motor insurance for the over fifties. The musical advertisements, however, range for all ages: a reading of *The Nutcracker* for children, the latest releases from young stars like Mae and opera singer Izzy for young adults, to Swedish Classics for the older readers. There is also a heavy emphasis on home and lifestyle; antiques, jewellery, wine and travel.

Both *Empire* and *Classic FM* employ free extras to draw the reader's interest further. *Empire* has a booklet of glossy pictures of some of 'the sexy 69' and *Classic FM* has a CD of violin prodigies. Both magazines reveal the best in advertisement publishing, for 'the publisher with the edge is the one who is fully aware of advertisers' needs and constantly monitors the relationship between those needs and the needs of the reader.'

Conclusion

Empire is visually brilliant; *Classic FM* visually pleasing. *Empire* concentrates on what's new, what's hot, with the odd tribute to a classic, whereas *Classic FM* holds onto past and tradition, whilst glancing at new blood. Both are complex magazines but inside the elements visually connect, as they should. The pages are well balanced and the subtle differences reveal harmony and contrast. The designers in either magazine use their own terms for creative flexibility. Whilst *Empire's* layout is ordered within boxes and rules, *Classic FM* relies on the advantages of white space, framing their

Media pack card from www.empireonline.com

John Wharton, *Managing Magazine Publishing*, p. 45.

articles with photographs. Then, whilst *Classic FM* maintains order with justification, *Empire* uses ranged-left type to avoid formality.

From my analysis of the design of these two magazines, the bottom line for any magazine is to identify the potential reader and put the message across. Representatives from both *Empire* and *Classic FM* both stressed that they keep clean, well up-to-date lists of their current and prospective readers. Design is vital in making this communication easier. A magazine must have a clear, direct design policy, as well as a good writing style and high production values, to meet the needs of its intended readership. The design, as well as the quality of the paper, binding and print will all affect the reader's attitude towards the publication. The key is for all these elements to work together to achieve the best possible result, topped by a competitive price.

Whilst a magazine may satisfy current demands, it may not satisfy in the future, which is why a magazine must be flexible enough to accept and manipulate change well. The *Empire* art director's word for the magazines is 'timely', justifiable for its eleven years on the shelves, whilst *Classic FM*, now in its seventh year, will continue to be strong as long as its radio station is listened to, winner of last year's UK Station of the Year.

It has recently proved it can adapt, as the letters of its warmly receiving audience reveal. These magazines have accepted change and their design skills have vastly contributed to their success, as they are used to effectively communicate with their readers. John Wharton sums up the key to success: 'The message is simple: provide readers and advertisers with what they need and want; constantly monitor the magazine's performance; and make sure there is no gap for someone else to come in and fill.'

John Wharton, *Managing Magazine Publishing*, pp. 53-4.

Bibliography

Apple, *Apple Programmer's introduction to the Apple IIGS* (Boston: Addison-Wesley, 1988).

de Bono, Edward, *The Five Day Course in Thinking* (London: Allen Lane, 1968).

Chicago Manual of Style, The, 14th Edition (Chicago: University of Chicago Press, 1993).

Cowen, Matthew, 'Hotline: an expert's view', *Campaign* (7 September 2001).

Gorkin, Baruch, and Tom Carnase, *The best in digital classic text fonts* (Graphis, 1995).

Goslett, Dorothy, *The Professional Practice of Design*, 3rd edition (London: Batsford, 1984).

Green, Phil, *Understanding digital colour* (Pittsburgh: Graphic Arts Technical Foundation, 1995).

Gregory, R.L., *Eye and Brain: the Psychology of Seeing*, 3rd edition (London: Weidenfeld & Nicholson, 1979).

Hurlbert, Allen, *Publication Design: A guide to page layout, typography, format and style* (Wokingham, Berkshire, Van Nostrand Reinhold, 1976).

Itten, Johannes, *The art of color: the subjective experience and objective rationale of color*, translated by Ernst von Haagen (New York: Van Nostrand Reinhold, 1973).

Leslie, Jeremy, *Issues: New Magazine Design* (London: Laurence King, 2000).

Linotype, *Linotype Collection: Typeface Handbook* (Cheltenham: Linotype Limited, 1989).

McLean, Ruari, (ed), *Typographers on Type: An Illustrated Anthology from William Morris to the Present Day* (London: Lund Humphries, 1995).

Neurath, Otto., *Basic by Isotype,* Psych Minatures General Series (London: Kegan Paul, 1936).

Neurath, Otto., *International picture language/Internationale Bildersprache,* a facsimile reprint of the 1936 English edition, forward by Robin Kinross, Psyche Miniatures General Series (London: Kegan Paul and the Department of Typography & Graphic Communication, University of Reading, 1980).

Poynor, Rick, *Typography Now: The Next Wave* (London: Booth-Clibborn Editions, 1991).

Ryle, Gilbert, *The Concept of Mind* (London: Hutchinson, 1949).

Sassoon, Rosemary, (ed), *Computers and Typography* (Oxford: Intellect, 1993).

Tschichold, Jan, *The New Typography: a handbook for modern designers,* translated by Ruari McLean (Los Angeles: University of California Press, 1998), p. 64.

Walker, Ronald, *Magazine Design: A Hands-On Guide* (London: Blueprint, 1992).

Walters, Marcus, *Your Future in Magazines: A Guide to Jobs in the Magazine Industry* (http://publishing.about.com/arts/publishing/cs/magazinelaunch/index.htm).

Warford, H.S., *Design for Print Production* (London and New York: Focal Press, 1971).

Wharton, John, *Managing Magazine Publishing* (London: Blueprint, 1992).

White, Jan V., *Designing for Magazines: Common Problems, Realistic Solutions* (New York: R. R. Bowker Co., 1982).

Williams, Robin, *The Non-Designer's Design Book* (Peachpit Press: California, 1994).

Index

M10777S